*Routledge Revivals*

# The Shipping Industry

First published in 1986, *The Shipping Industry* is a comprehensive study of the shipping industry. It shows how technological advances at the time in shipping design led to improved efficiency and the transportation of more sophisticated cargoes, promoting international trade. Analyzing the complex interplay between technological developments, economic pressures, and political forces that moulded the modern shipping industry into its form, the author offers students of transportation and economics, shipping industry trainees, and shipbrokers a better understanding of the key factors underlying the industry's growth and development.

# The Shipping Industry

## The Technology and Economics of Specialisation

Edmund J. Gubbins

Routledge
Taylor & Francis Group

First published in 1986
by Gordon and Breach Science Publishers

This edition first published in 2026 by Routledge
4 Park Square, Milton Park, Abingdon, Oxon, OX14 4RN

and by Routledge
605 Third Avenue, New York, NY 10158

*Routledge is an imprint of the Taylor & Francis Group, an informa business*



**Publisher's Note**
The publisher has gone to great lengths to ensure the quality of this reprint but points out that some imperfections in the original copies may be apparent.

**Disclaimer**
The publisher has made every effort to trace copyright holders and welcomes correspondence from those they have been unable to contact.

For Product Safety Concerns and Information please contact our EU representative GPSR@taylorandfrancis.com. Taylor & Francis Verlag GmbH, Kaufingerstraße 24, 80331 München, Germany

A Library of Congress record exists under LCCN: 85012605

ISBN: 978-1-041-29513-6 (hbk)
ISBN: 978-1-003-76992-7 (ebk)
ISBN: 978-1-041-29523-5 (pbk)

Book DOI 10.4324/9781003769927

# THE SHIPPING INDUSTRY

## The Technology and Economics of Specialisation

Edmund J. Gubbins
*Loughborough University of Technology, Loughborough, U.K.*

GORDON AND BREACH SCIENCE PUBLISHERS
New York · London · Paris · Montreux · Tokyo

Gordon and Breach Science Publishers

P.O. Box 786
Cooper Station
New York, NY 10276
United States of America

P.O. Box 197
London WC2E 9PX
England

58, rue Lhomond
75005 Paris
France

14-9 Okubo 3-chome
Shinjuku-ku
Tokyo 160
Japan

**Library of Congress Cataloging in Publication Data**

Gubbins, Edmund J., 1941-
The shipping industry.

(Transportation studies, ISSN 0278-3819; v. 5)
1. Shipping. I. Title. II. Series.
HE571.G8 1985 387.5′44 85-12605
ISBN 2-88124-063-1

# Contents

# Preface

A fundamental principle of life seems to be that, over any given period of time, developments tend to lead to greater specialisation. This is certainly true of the shipping industry.

I have been aware for a number of years of the need for a book that focuses on this specialisation, tracing the complex interaction of technological developments, economic pressures and political forces that have produced the modern shipping industry. It is hoped that an introductory book of this nature will stimulate readers to delve more deeply into this fascinating area of study.

A book such as this could not have been completed without the aid of numerous organisations and I gratefully acknowledge all such assistance. In particular, I wish to thank Professor Norman Ashford for his encouragement, Sonny Tolofari for his help in the research and Derek Glenister for the diagrams. Heartfelt thanks to my wife Anne for her forbearance, encouragement and help especially with proofreading, and to Vivien for her patience in typing and retyping the manuscript.

EDMUND GUBBINS

# 1 Introduction

## The Function of Shipping

There are few nations capable of producing all their material requirements. The majority must trade any surplus of a home produced commodity for a surplus commodity produced by another country. All attempt to trade surpluses with several other countries, (1) in order to fulfil all their citizens' needs and (2) to ensure continuation of supply by using a number of sources. As affluence increases, the trade develops into an exchange of desirable but non-essential commodities, thus a distinct pattern of trade relationships emerges globally with an attendant need to establish physical methods of exchange.

The major function of the shipping industry is to close the physical gap between trading nations by allowing the exchange of surplus commodities. This includes the transporting of raw materials such as iron ore from primary extracting sites to manufacturing centres, energy producing materials such as coal and oil to consuming countries, agricultural products such as grain from surplus areas to deficient areas and the products of manufacturing industry to consumer markets. This activity is performed worldwide and links all parts of the globe in a network of routes, some of which are highly developed and heavily trafficked, others used occasionally at certain times of the year.

The importance of the shipping industry can be gauged by the fact that approximately 90% of all international trade by weight and 85% by value spend a large part of its overall journey in a ship. However, it must be emphasized that shipping or sea transport is only one link in a complex chain stretching from producer to consumer and that lorries, trains, barges, pipelines and aeroplanes play a part, especially in the collection and distribution of the freight in both the country of origin and the country of destination. In certain areas and for certain commodities, these other forms of transport are in direct competition with shipping.

Water borne transport is the cheapest means of moving large quantities of any commodity over long distances although it is in the main far slower than other forms of transport. Table 1.1 indicates the relative costs of carrying commodities over distances of 200 and 2,000 miles by the four principal transport modes and the relationship between modal costs and shows the relative reduction in costs per ton/mile over distance.

As can be seen from Table 1.1, the largest relative reduction in costs with distance is in the air mode. However, these statistics do not take direct account of the value of the cargo which may give air the edge over other modes despite it being the most expensive. A high value cargo can sustain a relatively high freight rate without this cost affecting its eventual selling price. There are also commodities that gain market penetration by the much quicker delivery times achieved by air transport.

## Objectives of Shipping

The prime operating objective of shipping is to move passengers and freight from one place to another as safely, economically and reliably as possible in line with good practice. There are a variety of reasons why people choose to use a shipping company to carry their goods or themselves, any one of which will play a part in the decision making process. In the case of freight, it is to carry goods from the place of origin to a place where they will be of more value. The tenta-

TABLE 1.1
OPERATING COST TAPER
(Relative cost/ton mile)

| Mode | 200 miles | 2000 miles |
|---|---|---|
| Ship[a] | 100 | 60 |
| Rail | 200 | 180 |
| Lorry | 500 | 480 |
| Cargo Jet | 3500 | 1140 |

(*Source:* Compiled from O.E.C.D. data)
[a]Shipping cost 100 at 200 miles

tive theory behind this proposition is that a commodity is of more value once transported to where more work can be accomplished on it, or where it is finally sold to a consumer. It follows that a car sitting in the factory yard does not have as much value as one sitting in the showroom. Transport, therefore, adds the *utility of place* to most commodities. For the passenger the reasons may be far more complex. The sea voyage may be more expensive and slower than the competing mode but there may be personal reasons, such as fear of flying or the desire to treat the journey as a holiday, which make the person want to undertake a sea voyage.

A shipping manager must always remember this derived nature of the demand for shipping services. By *derived* is meant that consumers are using sea transport as a means of fulfilling other objectives. Apart from the case of passengers on a cruise whose aim is to undertake a unique form of holiday, sea transport is a means of satisfying some more important objective. This indicates that, although in practical terms the passenger rents a cabin and the shipper rents some hold space in the ship for the duration of the voyage, their actions are different. The passenger wishes to arrive at the destination in order to carry out business or leisure activities, the freight shipper wishes to sell his goods in an overseas market. The journey itself is something that could easily be foregone if some other means could be found of exacting the transfer of passengers and freight instantly between two places.

The desired arrival must be accomplished safely with the cargo undamaged and the passenger uninjured. The ship usually arrives according to a pre-arranged timetable or contract and the voyage is undertaken at an agreed cost to the customer. The mix of speed and comfort, which is usually termed the quality of service, will depend on the standard of service required by the customer and by the price he is willing to pay.

It must be emphasized again, that the ship voyage is generally only one part of the overall journey: it is the final destination that is most important to the customer and other modes of transport that are used to bring cargo to the ship and take it away at the end of the voyage. The wishes of customers must always be given consideration by shipping companies, especially in relation to changing working methods which must fit into the overall practices used in other forms of transport if the customers' desires are to be met. These involve the shipowner in designing handling equipment and package sizes that are compatible with handling and package sizes demanded by other modes.

## Trade Routes

The flow patterns superimposed on ocean maps in the pages of atlases, usually anotated with distances in nautical miles, depict the major shipping routes between continents: these patterns can only be a static representation of the situation at the time of publication or compilation. The route pattern followed by ships is far from static and many factors contribute to their dynamic nature.

Oceans are generally considered to be a transport way unimpeded by obstructions, where ships are able to travel in total freedom. The shipping industry has developed through this concept of freedom of the seas but this concept is rapidly changing under the force of the U.N. Law of the Seas Conferences which are having an effect on all users. The oceans are able to support large structures of enormous weight and size and present less frictional resistance than is felt by land based vehicles. However, vast structures pose their own problems.

Shipping routes are affected by both political and physical factors outside the control of the industry. Weather systems can generate wind forces that result in heavy seas which can cause damage or total loss to cargo, passengers, ships' crew and the ships' structure. Rough weather can cause the ship to reduce speed or take another route in the hope of avoiding the worst of the storms but make schedule-keeping difficult. Modern ships are expected to keep to schedule and various technologically based weather reporting and routing advice schemes have been developed to help the ships' crew avoid the very bad weather.

Advances in weather routing and position fixing systems by the application of electronics have reduced some of the physical hazards, but technological advances in ship design and construction have, through the ability to build larger and faster ships, added others. Large ships can no longer use many of the traditional trading routes or ports because the draft is greater than the depth of water available. Large tankers can no longer navigate through the North Sea, Dover

Strait or Malacca Strait or dock in many U.S. ports. An increased research effort into the nature and behaviour of the sea bed, tidal streams and ocean currents has resulted from the trend towards larger ships.

Political events have effects on both trade routes and operational practices, for example the closure of the Suez Canal completely changed the established body of thought on trade between the Indian Ocean and N.W. Europe. The discovery of new sources of raw materials, the changing relativities between economic activities in different parts of the world and the climatic effects on agricultural production all add to the dynamic nature of the trade route pattern worldwide.

## World Trade

Table 1.2 shows the steady rise in the volume of world trade since the mid-nineteenth century. The rise has been greater or smaller according to the state of the world economy, but shows an almost continuous expansion.

Table 1.3 shows the growth of the world shipping fleet over the same timescale and this too shows a steady increase to meet the demands of world trade.

These tables do not give a complete picture of the relationships between world trade growth and world fleet size as the shipping industry is very vulnerable to the cycles of world economic activity. This is only to be expected in an industry that has as its main objectives the transportation of materials and manufactured goods between countries. In times of economic slump, trade between nations falls, thus reducing the demand for shipping services. This means that the shipping industry passes, as does the world economy, through cycles of slump and boom, so must ensure that the profits earned in times of boom are sufficient to enable it to survive through times of slump. The cycle necessitates there being at one time a scarcity of tonnage, at others a surplus. The situation is reflected in the freight rates that shipping companies can expect to earn, high in times of scarcity, low in times of surplus.

A number of factors must be highlighted when discussing World Trade and Fleet Growth as all statistics have inherent weaknesses

TABLE 1.2
WORLD TRADE
(million tonnes)

| | |
|---|---|
| 1850 | 50 |
| 1900 | 200 |
| 1939 | 520 |
| 1950 | 575 |
| 1960 | 1020 |
| 1970 | 2482 |
| 1975 | 3047 |
| 1980 | 3648 |
| 1982 | 3213 |

(*Sources:* O.E.C.D. Maritime Transport)

TABLE 1.3
WORLD FLEET
(million GRT)

| | |
|---|---|
| 1850 | 7 |
| 1900 | 28 |
| 1939 | 65.6 |
| 1950 | 84.5 |
| 1960 | 120 |
| 1970 | 227.5 |
| 1979 | 413 |
| 1982 | 424.7 |

(*Sources:* Lloyds Register: Statistical Tables)

when attempting to illustrate any given situation. The real measure of demand for shipping must take into account ship speed increases, advances in port handling techniques leading to reduced turn-round times, changing economic activities which alter route lengths, ship size changes which take advantage of economies of scale and technological advances in ship design and construction. These factors combined will have a large impact on ship productivity.

The change from sail to power driven ships, though phased over a long period, enabled ships to escape from the major delays imposed by the weather which in turn consolidated the establishment of scheduled services running to a set timetable. Shipping gradually polarised into scheduled liner service companies and whole voyage charters, known as tramping. The liner trades changed the management style in shipping companies by highlighting the need for fleet management as opposed to management of each individual ship. Fleet management, based in an office in the home port, was further enhanced by the introduction of radio. It was no longer necessary for the owners and managers of shipping fleets to rely on their ships masters for information and negotiations over cargo rates on the return leg of the voyage. This fact, almost unnoticed at the time, changed the vital role that the Master played in company affairs to that of the manager of the shipping system, chiefly concerned with the safe and efficient navigation of the ship from port to port.

The replacement of wood by iron, and later mild steel, for the construction of ships' hulls enabled lighter, stronger and larger ships to be built which combined with continuous improvements in the efficiency of the engine enabled increases in the payload for a given size of ship. The increased payload/displacement ratio resulted in large gains in productivity for individual ship voyages.

The major growth in the transport of petroleum products between 1913 and 1939 established the role of the oil tanker. In this period the world tanker fleet expanded by a factor of approximately 7.5. The quickening pace of technological change in ship design and construction over the past thirty years has resulted in the size of oil tankers rising from 60,000 dwt to over 500,000 dwt. The total size of the world fleet has not grown at the same rate as world trade. This reflects the increased productivity of the industry.

## Specialisation

A fundamental principle seems to be that over any given time period, industrial developments tend to lead to greater specialisation. This is certainly true of the shipping industry.

Figure 1 illustrates this principle by showing the developments of ship types over time. In the main all developments have moved towards the highly specialised portion of the diagram reflecting the greater productivity to be gained from a ship designed to carry a particular type of cargo.

There was very little to distinguish one ship from another in 1900 except the obvious differences between powered and sailing ships (although even at that time many powered ships had auxiliary sails). In fact, until the 1950's, there were very few surface features to differentiate the cargo liner from the tramp. The first specialised ship to evolve, apart from the passenger liner, was the oil tanker but even these ships were designed to carry most grades of oil. It is only in very recent times that the oil tanker has evolved into separate ships designed specifically to carry crude oil, products, chemicals, lubricating oil and gas. Each of these types is designed to operate within a particular sector of the market.

The all purpose tramp has been partially replaced by the bulk carrier which like its oil tanker counterpart, has become increasingly more specialised in the range of goods carried. The cargo liner has been superseded by the container ship, the barge carrier and the Roll on Roll off vessel.

Increasing diversification has profound effects on the shipping industry leading to a change in the nature of the management of shipping companies. As ships become more specialised, it becomes increasingly difficult to find employment outside a specific sector of the world economy. Each new ship type is designed to carry cargo marginally more effectively than the ship type it replaces. Managements must now consider much longer-term planning in order to find employment over the life of their investment fully and avoid, if possible, technological obsolescence for their ships.

The trend towards specialisation has prompted some shipowners and builders to investigate, design and build multi-purpose vessels which can trade across the specialist boundaries. The major type, the combination carrier, (see Figure 1.1) is designed to be able to carry both dry and liquid bulk cargoes.

## The Industry

The central focus of the shipping industry must be the ship. It is by operating ships that freight and passengers are transported from place to place and by the fares and freight rates paid for this service that returns on investment are made. It is the ship that enables world trade to be undertaken. By solving design and construction problems, naval architects have been able to provide the means of fulfilling the need to transport ever more complex and hazardous commodities across the seas.

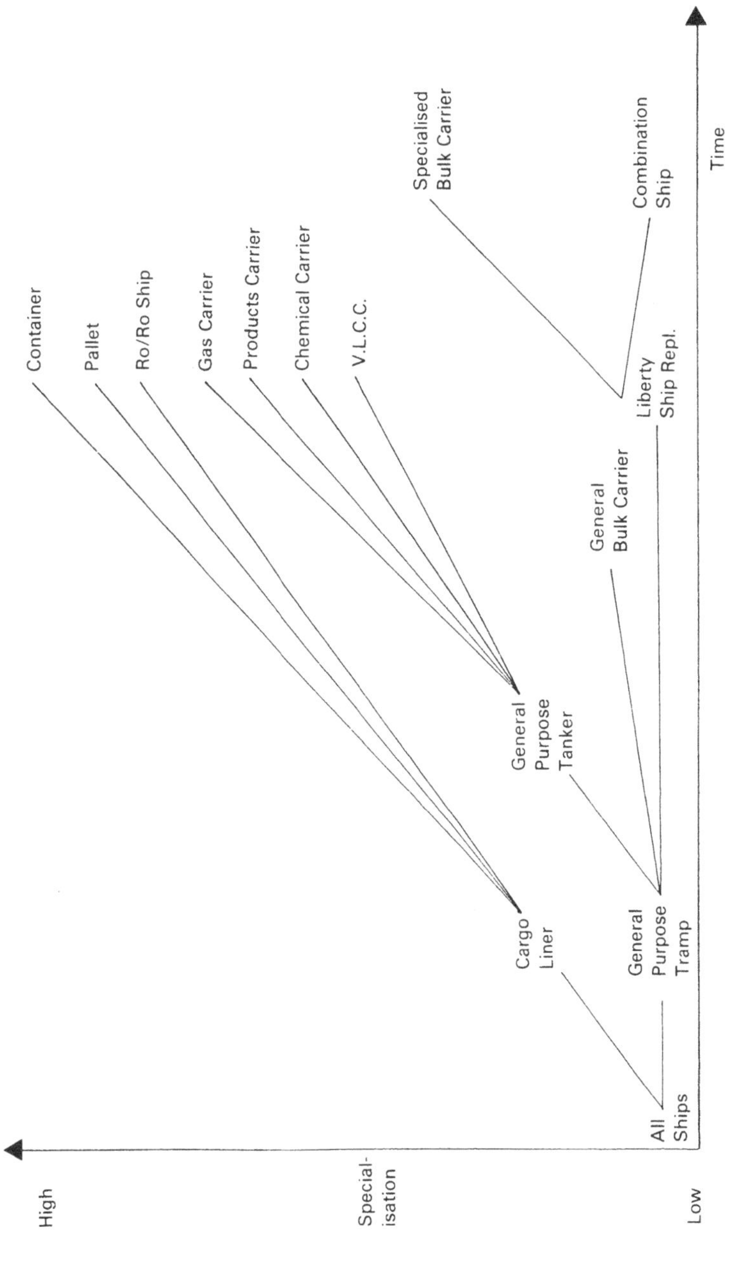


FIGURE 1.1. Ship specialisation over time

The purpose of this book is to introduce students, shipping industry trainees and persons interested to the shipping industry by concentrating on the various ship types that have evolved and the economic and technical reasons for their evolution.

## The Economic Reasons

These are mainly concerned with making the system more efficient by increasing the productivity of the component parts. The term *system* is used because it is often factors outside the control of the shipping company that must be changed in order to increase the productivity of the ship itself. Economies of scale play a large role in producing cheaper transport. However, in shipping, economies of scale can generally only be utilised if the port and inland transport systems are better designed. The biggest blockage to gaining from scale economies is the inability to increase the speed of cargo handling in port.

## The Technical Reasons

These concern the need to carry products safely and efficiently. Different commodities require the solution of a number of problems if they are to be carried successfully and only advances in technological research has enabled certain commodities to be handled and carried safely.

It must now be apparent that the type of ship used on any given trade route depends upon the type of commodity to be transported, how the commodity is packaged, the handling equipment available in ports at each end of the route, the inland transport mode used for on going delivery and the development stage reached by the countries in which the ports are situated. All these factors combine to form the parameters of choice when considering the shipping system.

With this last thought in mind, there are various ways in which the industry can be divided up for the purposes of study. In many modes of transport it is the custom to divide the industry between own account companies (those carrying their own goods in their own vehicles) and hire and reward operations. It is very difficult to make

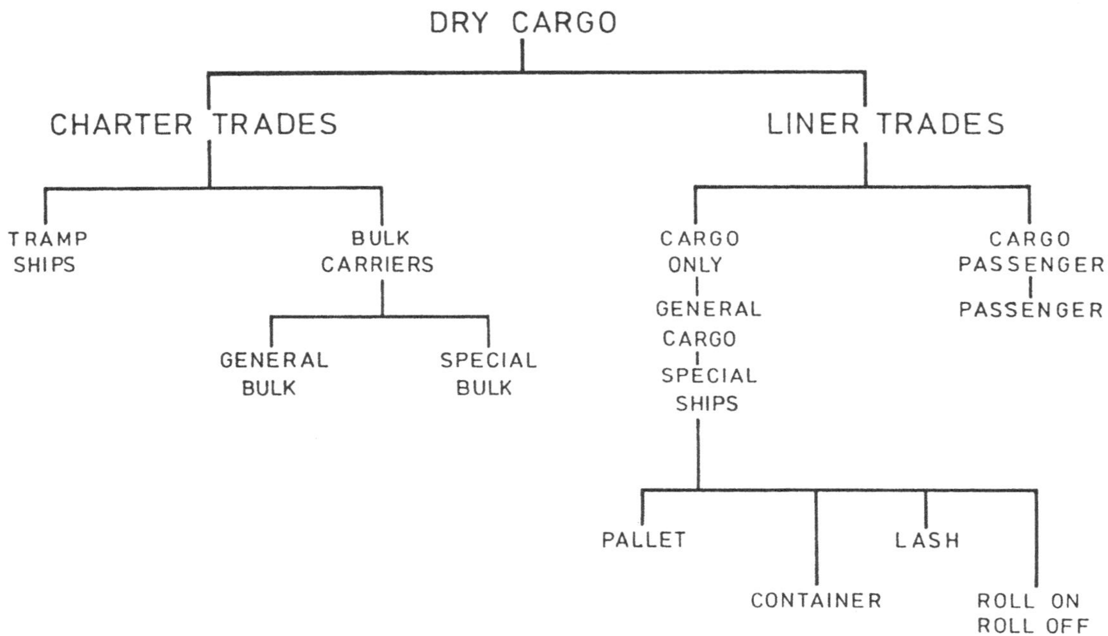


FIGURE 1.2. Outline of dry cargo trades

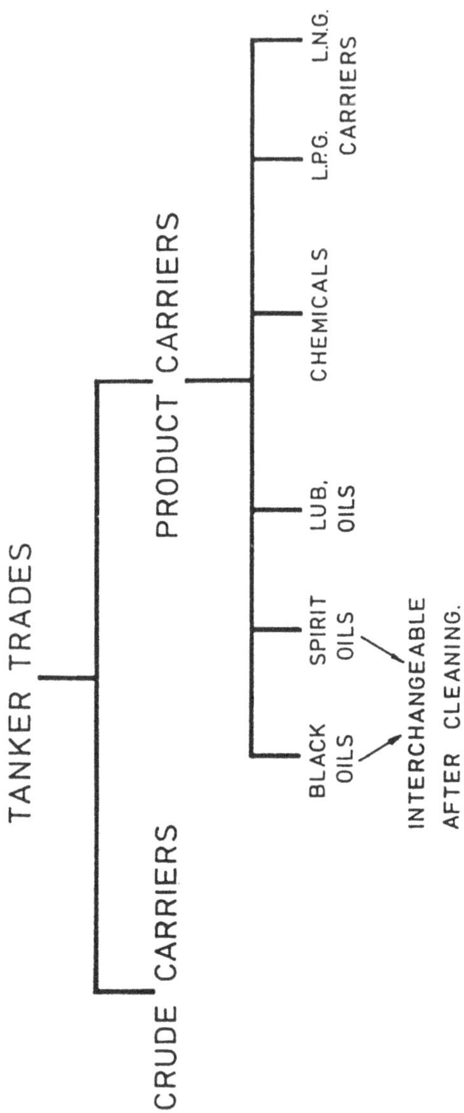


FIGURE 1.3. Outline of tanker trades

this distinction in shipping although in some sectors of the industry, there are a number of own account operators.

The second method is to divide according to the type of service performed that is between scheduled operations and contract hire services. In this book I have divided the industry up in this way though first I have split into market areas, namely dry and liquid cargo. Each of these market areas is then subdivided as in Figures 1.2 and 1.3 to illustrate the ship types giving an indication of the market sector within which each operates. It must be noted that the combination carrier does not appear on either diagram as this type of ship provides a link between one area and the other.

A further reading list which will help the student follow a particular aspect in depth is included at the end of each chapter.

## FURTHER READING

Abrahamsson, B.J., *International Ocean Shipping*, West-view Press, Colorado, 1980.

Alderton, P.M., *Sea Transport Operations and Economics*, Thomas Read, London, 1980.

Branch, A.E., *Elements of Shipping*, Chapman and Hall, London, 1981.

Couper, A.D., *Geography of Sea Transport*, Hutchinson, London.

Lawrence, S.A., *International Sea Transport — The Years Ahead*, Lexington Books, Massachusetts, 1972.

O.E.C.D., *Maritime Transport*, O.E.C.D. Paris (Annually).

O'Loughlin, *The Economics of Sea Transport*, Pergamon, London, 1967.

Rinman, J. and R. Linden, *Shipping — How it Works*, Rinman and Linden, Gothenburg, 1979.

# 2 Cargo Liners

## Break Bulk Cargo Trades

The growth of world trade during the second half of the nineteenth century, created a desire on the part of manufacturing companies for regular and frequent shipping services to fulfil the needs of their export markets. Exporters needed regular services to maintain a steady flow of deliveries to their customers, demanding that small parcels of high value goods be delivered on pre-determined dates in order to minimise the need to hold large stocks of a product in the importing country to satisfy the demand. Reduced stockholding helped to minimise costs and enabled producers to streamline their production schedules. To fit into this pattern of marketing products, the shipper needed to have advanced knowledge not only of sailing times but of the likely freight in order to price his product in the export area.

The cargo liner was developed to meet these needs, often being designed to serve a particular trade route for a specific range of products and commodities. The ship operates over an advertised course to a planned timetable, carrying parcels of cargo from several shippers in order to fill the ship's payload spaces. Usually, the vessels are grouped into fleets operated by large companies and the fleet operator has the difficult task of catering for the varying needs of a number of shippers within the confines of one ship and on the same voyage.

The individual fleet size and ship size will depend on a number of factors, the major one being the service frequency which is often controlled by shipper requirements for that route and the amount of cargo needing to be transported at any particular time.

## Conferences

A parallel development to liner shipping was the growth of shipping conferences. These organizations are associations of companies serving a given route, set up with the intention of protecting the scheduled operator from competition by non-scheduled operators. It is argued that to maintain a scheduled service, the shipowner has to accept lower load factors (the ratio of actual cargo carried to the designed cargo carrying capacity of the ship) than would be the case if ships only sailed when enough cargo had accumulated to make the voyage viable. A scheduled service is maintained throughout the year whether there is sufficient cargo for economic operation or not. The profit margins of the operator are maintained over a year by cross subsidising revenues between periods of high demand and low demand, that is earning surplus profits in one period to pay for likely losses in other periods. The non-scheduled operator would be able to under cut the scheduled operator on a particular trade route during periods of high demand, then leave that trade route when demand fell. The scheduled operator would then inherit the problems of operation at times of low demand. There is also the argument that exporters need notice of freight rate changes to price their products and the conference system can have a steadying effect on freight rates over lengthy periods. Finally, conferences claim they help world trade by subsidising between high value goods and low value goods. This is achieved by charging differential rates based on the ability of a product to absorb the transport cost in the final selling price. By this mechanism low value goods continue to flow around the world even though the freight rate charged is not economic. Shipping conferences are, therefore, bodies that share out the trade between component companies and fix the freight rate to be charged.

National Governments and fleet owners in developing countries feel that the conference system descriminates against their shipping fleets and export trades. In the traditional maritime countries Shippers Councils have been established to provide some counter balance against the powerful conferences but many shipping people in developing countries feel that they have neither the influence nor power to control conferences. At a meeting in Geneva in March 1974, the United Nations Conference on Trade and Development (UNCTAD) adopted an international convention, called the Code of

Conduct for Liner Conferences, which aims to regulate the world's liner traffic and give greater opportunities for developing countries to set up and run their own fleets.

### The Code of Conduct for Liner Conferences

*The objectives and principles of the code* The contracting parties to the Convention to the Code desired to improve the liner conference system, recognized the need for a universally acceptable code of conduct for liner conferences and have taken into account the special needs and problems of the developing countries with respect to the activities of liner conferences serving their foreign trade. The Code has three fundamental objectives:

- to facilitate the orderly expansion of world seaborne trade;
- to stimulate the development of regular and efficient liner services adequate to the requirements of the trade concerned;
- to ensure a balance of interests between suppliers and users of liner shipping services;

and three underlying principles;

- that conference practices should not involve any discrimination against shipowners, shippers or the foreign trade of any country;
- that conferences hold meaningful consultations with shippers' organizations, shippers' representatives and shippers on matters of common interest with, upon request, the participation of appropriate authorities;
- that conferences should make available to interested parties pertinent information about their activities which are relevant to those parties and should publish meaningful information on their activities.

*Structure* The 'Final Act of the United Nations Conference of Plenipotentiaries on a Code of Conduct for Liner Conferences' is itself merely a detailed list of which governments and other bodies were represented at the proceedings and a referral to the accompanying 'Convention on a Code of Conduct for Liner Conferences', and other resolutions adopted. There is also a list of states whose representatives had signed the Act.

Annex I to the Final Act contains the Convention which gives full details of the mandatory provisions of the Code. It sets out the Objectives and Principles and contains 54 Articles presented in seven chapters. References to 'the Code' usually refer to the contents of the Convention.

Annex II to the Final Act contains three resolutions which are not mandatory.

## Major Issues Covered by the Code (Convention)

*Conference membership* Conferences are bound, under the Code, to accept as members liners from the countries whose trade the Conference serves, and should accept third-countries' lines as long as this does not result in overtonnaging of the route. It is basically a system of 'open' membership for trading partners and 'closed' membership for third countries. All applicants are required to give evidence of their ability and intention to operate a regular, adequate and efficient service on a long-term basis.

*Cargo sharing* The so-called 40-40-20 provision is not actually set out as specifically as such a title suggests. The Code states that the national shipping lines of the two trading partners should have "equal rights" to participate in the freight and volume of traffic generated, and that third-country lines should have the right to acquire "a significant part, such as 20 per cent".

*Adequacy of service* Conferences are obliged to ensure that their members provide a regular, adequate and efficient service of the required frequency, avoiding bunching and gapping of sailings.

*Fighting ships* These are strictly prohibited.

*Freight rates* Freight rates shall be fixed at as low a level as is commercially feasible whilst permitting a reasonable profit, and should not unfairly differentiate between similarly situated shippers. Tariffs should be drawn up as simply and clearly as possible and shippers kept adequately informed of the situation. The Code tightly controls the altering of freight rates: suitable notice (as specified) must be given to shippers along with justification for any increase. There seems to be little scope for flexibility — rates cannot just be altered to match costs without going through a rather tedious procedure.

*Information for shippers* Conferences, which have traditionally been excessively secretive, are obliged under the Code to keep shippers informed on freight rates, disputes, etc. Also, shippers have a fair amount of power invested in them and conferences are obliged to consult them over anything that is in their interest to know.

*Loyalty agreements* Conferences are left free to draw up loyalty agreements with shippers: not even the deferred rebate system is outlawed.

*Conciliation machinery* The Code gives a detailed account of who should take part in the conciliation process, but very little practical guidance on how to reconcile differences of opinion.

*Denunciation* Any Contracting Party is free to denounce the Code once it has been in force for two years, so it could be used merely for short-term advantage without being inhibited by any longer-term commitment.

The Code is a fairly comprehensive document, although it cannot claim to be exhaustive. It is also fairly precise in most areas: 'reasonable' periods (for notification etc.) are clearly specified, but with provision for custom and practice to be observed where this differs significantly from the period stated. However, there are also areas of flexibility, e.g. the 40-40-20 provision. It is easy to criticize the Code for being too rigid or too flexible in respect to different issues, but it should be credited with being the first widely accepted document on international seaborne shipping and as such had no past experience to draw on. It is quite a good first attempt.

*Entry into force* On the 6th April 1983 West Germany ratified the Convention to the Code and the Netherlands acceded to it. This meant that a total of 28.67% of the relevant world liner tonnage (from Lloyd's Register of Shipping 1973) had been brought under the jurisdiction of the Code. Thus, both the conditions for its entry into force had been fulfilled — more than 25% of world liner grt, represented by more than 24 countries had subscribed to the instrument. Consequently, the Code of Conduct entered into force six months later, on the 6th October 1983.

*The authority of the code* Many countries — some of them quite powerful ones like the USA, South Africa and Brazil — are not Contracting Parties to the Code and are unlikely to become so; thus its sphere of influence is limited. This effect is compounded by the free-trade agreement of the EEC and the possible extension of this to other OECD countries.

The Code does not explicitly apply to anything except liner conferences and their operations — although UNCTAD is under pressure to extend its principles to all shipping.

Thus, the global effect of the Code is unlikely to be as momentous as its critics have feared and proponents hoped for. There is currently much anxiety over how to translate the Code into practice, and there is doubt over its enforceability, so it is possible that it may flounder before it really has a chance to achieve anything.

*The code as a tool for development* The Code was devised as aid to developing countries, and so, in the absence of massively expanded world trade, developed countries were bound to lose out where developing countries gained.

It has taken twenty years for the Code to be translated from a vague dissatisfaction with liner conferences to the entry into force of a precise document. The world has not stood still in the meantime; many developing countries, being impatient of waiting for the introduction of international regulation, have taken unilateral action to protect and expand their shipping interests. In several cases the Code has been superseded by more stringent conditions which benefit the developing country more than the Code would so there is no incentive to adopt the provisions of the Code. For the developing countries who wish to expand their liner operations but have not adopted this approach, or have been less successful, the Code will be beneficial. In both cases the losers are the traditional maritime nations (i.e. developed countries). There is also a possibility that the Code will be enlisted as legalized protection for infant fleets, only to be denounced when the fleets are strong enough to survive without it (or when different forms of protection seem more beneficial).

*The code and free trade* The Code is inherently restrictive, although this is considered acceptable as it deters the proliferation of tighter restrictions. However, when in a competitive situation a restricted conference may lose out to unrestricted non-conference operations. Thus, an 'outsider' may have a competitive edge over a 'codist' conference, and the conference may end up in economic difficulties. Admittedly, conferences can offer favourable terms to regular customers via loyalty agreements, but such an advantage may not be good enough as outsiders may simply undercut the standard rate so that all shippers move their cargoes at the lower rate.

*Long-term effects* In the long-term, any effects of the Code will probably pale into insignificance beside the other changes that are occurring in the liner shipping sector. The fleets of most other developed countries have been declining sharply in recent years and the Code — if it has any real effect — will tend to encourage this trend.

The Code as an institution will encourage open-management, but may nurture bureaucracy and its formal requirements may limit the competitiveness of conferences. This could add to the threat to the very existence of the conference system.

The conference system is in the process of being radically reformed to suit the commercial climate of the 1980s. The UNCTAD Code of Conduct for Liner Conferences has taken nearly 10 years to be introduced, and is based on ideas conceived 15 or 20 years ago; it is unlikely to have the tremendous impact that it would have had if introduced much earlier as it merely reinforces trends which have been occurring anyway and is irrelevant in other areas. The Code is fast becoming an anachronism.

## Liner Fleet

It is interesting to note that the size of the world liner fleet has not grown as quickly as world trade which points to a rise in productivity of the individual units. There are other factors that are important. Many commodities once carried by cargo liner are aggregated into shipments large enough to fill a whole ship and are carried commercially in bulk carriers. Two examples will suffice to illustrate this point. At one time, grain was carried in small parcels in cargo liners: it is now carried in full ships loads on voyage contracts. Automobiles were also a stable product but many large shippers of these have designed and built special car carrying ships.

## Cargo Liners

The conventional cargo liner (see Figure 2.1) is a multi-deck ship with many individual cargo compartments to accommodate small parcels of different commodities. The main features may differ in lay-out and use of the cargo spaces according to the particular trade route for which the ship is designed. Some liners have refridgerated cargo spaces with many decks but long holds to carry the greatest amount of cargo whilst allowing plenty of free circulation of air. Refridgerated cargoes are not all the same and require a range of temperatures from +13°C for bananas to −26°C for shell fish. These ships must be fitted with the right equipment to maintain the required environment in the holds.

Tanks are built into some hold space, providing the ship with the capability of carrying small parcels of special oils. These tanks are designed for the carriage of both liquid or dry cargo or, if necessary, water ballast. The entrance must, therefore, be large enough to allow parcels of general cargo to be loaded while at the same time capable of being made liquid tight when carrying oils. In many cases heating coils have to be used to keep the oil viscous; the ship must also have equipment to provide heating and to pump the oil when discharging.

Heavy lifts are often handled by shore based cranes but most cargo liners are fitted with some form of heavy lift derrick to handle heavy items of cargo in those ports where shore based equipment is not available. There is a marked trend for heavy lifts to be handled by specialised heavy lift ships especially on routes where there is sufficient traffic to make the utilisation of these ships economic.

The dimensions of the individual ship are governed by the limits imposed by the ports along the route and flexibility requires that the ship is able to operate to a large number of ports. Any increase in size tends to reduce the number of ports at which the ship can call. The ship's dimensions have effects on the port's ability to accommodate

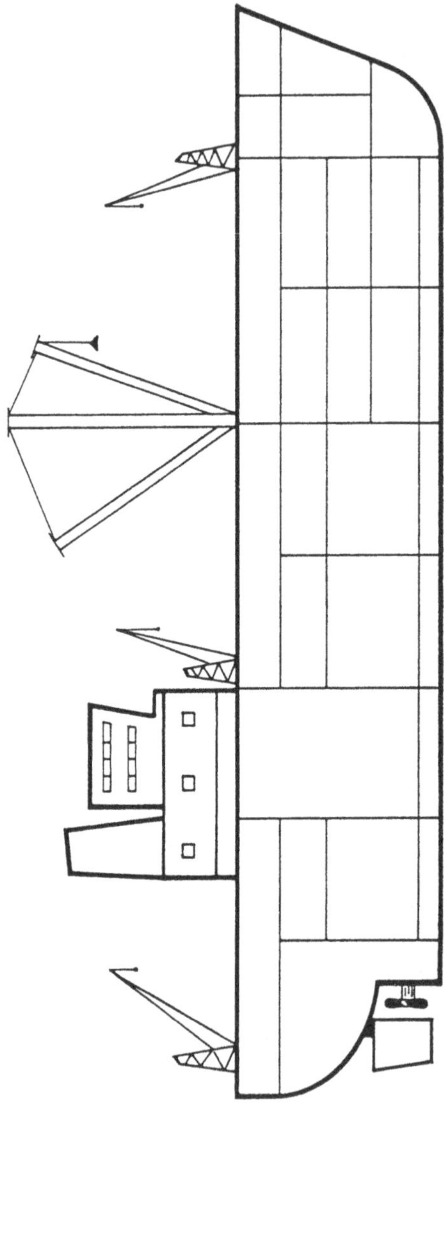

FIGURE 2.1. Conventional cargo liner

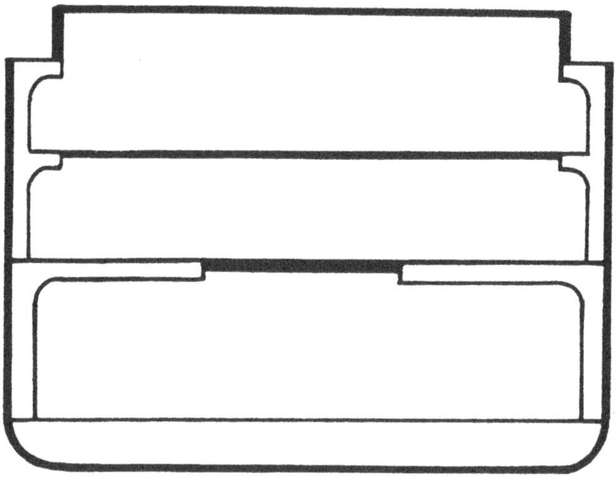

FIGURE 2.2. Transverse section through conventional cargo liner hold

the vessel but the limiting factor is very often the beam which is closely limited by physical structures such as canal and lock widths.

In general, the cargo liner is designed to carry cargo having a large volume to weight ratio. This ratio is generally known as the *stowage factor* and is expressed in terms of cubic feet per ton or cubic metres per tonne. Most commodities with a stowage factor of between 40 and 50 cubic feet per ton will load the ship to her design draft with all cargo spaces full (for a full explanation of stowage factors see Chapter 5). Most cargo liner freight stows at more than 50 and therefore the ships rarely reach their design draft.

Liner services serve a multitude of shippers on any one voyage to a number of ports along the route. The ship sails to a set timetable, leaving port at the advertised time whether there is sufficient cargo on board to make the voyage profitable or not. The ships must be very flexible in their arrangements of holds to take account of the various conditions in which they sail. If the itinerary includes a number of discharge ports, the cargo must be stowed such that at each port the required cargo can be handled without disturbing cargo destined for ports further along the route. At the same time, the ship must have adequate stability, the correct trim and the cargo must be stowed so that it does not shift at any stage of the voyage.

This flexibilty must be extended to the cargo handling gear. Along most trade routes the ship will meet a mixture of port environments, some with very modern shore based cargo handling equipment which makes any equipment on the ship redundant, while at others the ship will discharge at berths with only rudimentary equipment — indeed in some ports the ship will be anchored and the cargo discharged using ships gear into barges. The problem of cargo handling can be overcome by fitting the ship with equipment that is designed to meet all the conditions encountered on a particular route.

Cargo liners are fitted with a mixture of derricks and cranes; there are advantages and disadvantages attached to each of these systems. Derricks are usually used in the "union purchase" mode (see Figure 2.2) which means that one derrick is fixed to plumb the hold and the other to plumb the quay. The derrick runners are fixed together at the hook and the discharge is accomplished by one runner taking the weight until the set is above the hatch combing, gradually transferring the weight from one runner to the other until the set is over the quay and then landing the cargo using the second runner. Cranes have advantages in that they can be slewed to spot a parcel of cargo in any part of the hold for hooking on to the runner, the hook cycle is faster and cranes can usually lift heavier loads. Crane operators need more training, the cranes have appreciably higher capital and maintenance costs, put additional top weight on to the ship which affects the stability and need very wide hatch openings to reap the full advantages of their flexibility.

## Economies of Scale

Very little change took place in break bulk shipping until the nineteen sixties, the size of ship did not increase in the same way as the tanker and the bulk carrier nor did its method of operation.

Economies of scale in shipping can be stated quite simply although the subject is more complex than the explanation used here. Large ships are less costly to operate at sea per ton of cargo carried because crew, fuel, capital and maintenance costs do not increase in the same proportion as the cargo carrying capacity. Costs in port tend, however, to increase with size for any given handling rate as it takes longer to discharge a greater volume of cargo.

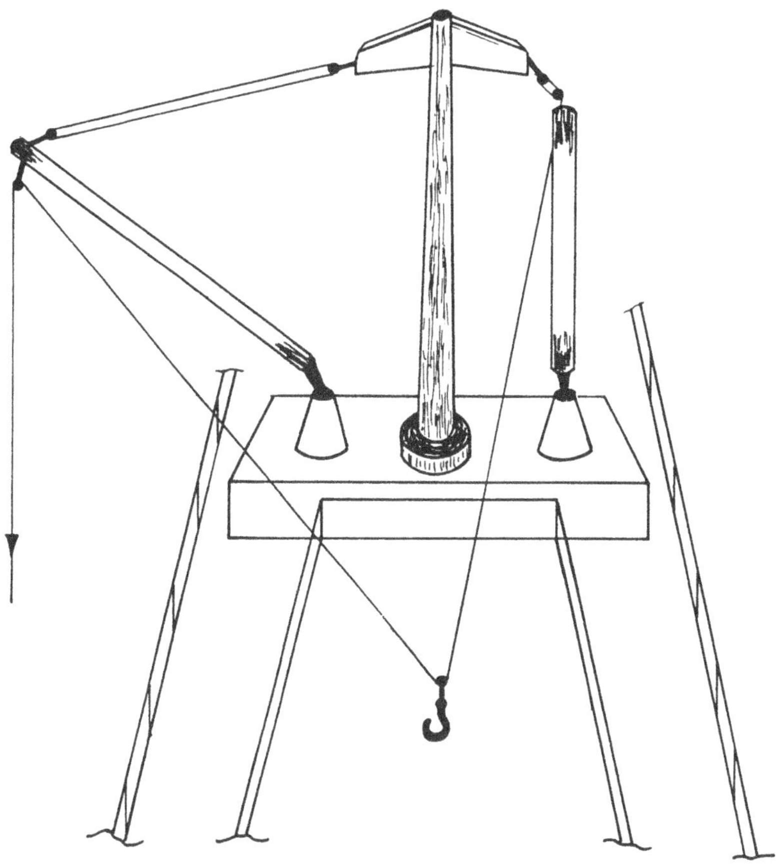

FIGURE 2.3. Union purchase

In break bulk shipping any increase in ships size tends to lead to a proportionate increase in the time spent in port. However, although in most branches of the shipping industry cargo handling rates generally improve with increases in ships length, there are severe restrictions placed in the way of improvements in the general cargo sector. The ability to reach the cargo with the handling gear can be taken as a function of ships length in that more sets of equipment can be used the longer the ship and the greater number of holds. One problem in break bulk shipping is that the ability to reach the cargo increases at a much slower rate than the amount of cargo to be handled. Deadweight or cubic capacity tends to increase with the cube of length and there may be restrictive practices on the part of stevedores that make it impossible to take full advantage of the better accessibility.

It has been found that on average, a general cargo ship spends more time in port than at sea and that over 55% of all operating costs can be said to accrue in port. Of these, the most important are the direct port costs — cargo handling charges and port dues.

Conventional cargo handling is very labour intensive and time consuming both in port and throughout the rest of the transport chain. The transportation of general cargo involves the handling of a large number of small parcels packaged in a variety of forms — bags, boxes, bales and cartons all of different shapes and sizes. Very often different forms of packaging need different handling equipment which leads to delays while equipment is changed during the handling process.

Cargo arrives in the port on various forms of transport — trucks, rail wagons or barges and is placed in a transit shed for sorting into destination port loads, loading order and compatibility with other commodities. The cargo is taken from the transit shed in load order, assembled into sets at the ship's side, lifted into the ship's hold and stowed in position ready for the voyage. Although this process necessitates a large amount of brute force, a great deal of skill is demanded to ensure that cargo is stowed so that damage does not occur in transit.

The cargo must be stowed throughout the ship in such a way that three criteria are satisfied:

- the ship must maintain adequate stability throughout the voyage even after partial discharge of the cargo
- the cargo is stowed so that it can be discharged at a number of ports with as little shifting of cargo destined for subsequent ports as possible
- the cargo remaining after part discharge is stowed so that it will not shift during the voyage between ports.

## Problems of General Cargo Handling

Stevedoring and port costs rose rapidly in the nineteen fifties and sixties due mainly to rapid increases in wage costs for stevedores, port congestion resulting from a lack of investment in infrastructure and higher port dues. Shipowners had traditionally passed on these increases to their customers in the form of higher freight rates or temporary surcharges for using certain ports. In the early nineteen sixties increases in freight rates to take account of rising port costs met with resistance from shippers and certain national governments forcing shipowners to improve the ships in-port performance in order to increase productivity and stabilise costs.

Ships were designed with flush hatch coverings in the holds to facilitate the use of fork lift trucks, thus cutting into the need for high cost labour and speeding up the handling process. Advances in ship building techniques led to ships designed with very wide hatch openings while retaining the strength requirements of the structure, and, combining these wide hatches with the extensive use of ships cranes, the manhandling of cargo into the centre of the hatch was reduced thus helping to further speed up the handling process. Cargo was strapped to a pallet forming a rigid unit and stowed in the hold using the fork truck. Bags of cargo were slung so that the slings were left in the hold and only had to be hooked on when discharging. Steel hatch covers capable of being handled by one man replaced boards and tarpaulins, making the opening and closing of hatches less time consuming and labour intensive.

It was realized that these new methods of cargo handling and ship design were only having a marginal effect on ship productivity. What was clearly required was a complete re-think about the methods used to handle cargo throughout the transport chain. Any system developed had to improve the productivity of the ship by cutting drastically the time spent by the ship in port.

## Cargo Unitisation

Unitisation involves the packaging of a number of small items of cargo into a standard size unit that can be handled by specifically designed mechanical aids. This has the effect of reducing the labour content and speeding up the handling of goods.

The major methods developed to fulfil these principles use different unitising techniques. Containerisation involves the packing of cargo into boxes of a standard size as early in the transport chain as possible. Boxes of standard size can easily be transferred between modes without disturbing the cargo inside. Roll on Roll off utilises the ability of cargo packed on trailers to be hauled onto and off the ship via a ramp or bridge using either the inland transport power unit or a tractive unit supplied by the port. Pallets are widely used in distribution and ships have been designed to load these through side doors using fork lift trucks. Barge carrying systems connect places with extensive inland waterway networks — full barges are loaded onto the ship thus disconnecting the cargo handling and sea transport components.

These systems have been developed to overcome some of the problems associated with break bulk shipping and are now used globally. However, they have not replaced the conventional ship. The description of break bulk shipping in this chapter still applies in many parts of the world.

## FURTHER READING

Bram, P.B., *Cargo Handling and the Modern Port*, Pergamon Press Ltd., London, 1965.

Chappell, D., Marine Transport Centre, Liverpool University, 1977.

Deakin, B.M., *Shipping Conferences: A Study of Their Origins, Developments and Economic Practices*, Cambridge University Press, 1973.

J.J. Henry Co., Inc., *Next Generation Cargo Liner. Phase 1 Final Report*, PB 297 590, MA-RD 940 79066, U.S. Government, Washington, 1979.

Kummerman, H. and R. Jacunet, *Ships Cargo — Cargo Ships*, MacGregor Publications, London, 1979.

Rochdale, Viscount, The Committee of Inquiry into Shipping Cmmd 4337, H.M.S.O., 1970. (For *Liner Shipping* — Chapter 7).

Ryder, S.C., *Optimal Speed and Ship Size in the Liner Trades*, 1978.

Sletmo, S.K., and E.W. Williams, *Liner Conference in the Container Age*, MacMillan Publishing Co. Inc., New York, 1980.

Sturmey, S.G., *Shipping Economics*, MacMillan Press Ltd., London, 1975.

# 3 Containerisation

The reasons for the development of cargo unitisation were discussed in Chapter 2 and it was explained that most people concerned with international break bulk cargo carriage felt that the through transport cost to the shipper had to be reduced or stabilised if the shipping industry was to meet the needs of international trade. One way to accomplish this reduction, (applied to break bulk shipping) is to use the same underlying principles of handling that are used in the bulk cargo area in the movement of general cargo. This means handling homogeneous cargoes by mechanical handling equipment in as near a constant flow as possible. This, in turn, means consolidating small individual packages of cargo into standard units and designing the handling equipment to move them without disturbing the individual packages.

The container system provides the opportunity to manipulate standard units of cargo by highly mechanical means throughout the journey from first packing place to final destination. There is an opportunity to make large cost savings in through transport costs by standardising the methods of carriage and transfer between modes. Essentially, the goods are packed into large boxes providing protection from the weather and bad handling throughout their transit. The boxes can be transferred between modes efficiently and quickly.

## Advantages of Containerisation

There are large gains in productivity by the shipping company when using containers to transport goods when compared to the performance of break bulk services. It takes efficient organization to reap the benefits inherent in greater use of mechanical equipment and any efficient container service must utilise the equipment fully. The most costly item of equipment in the through transport system is the ship but the productivity needed to earn returns on this investment is to a large extent outside the control of the shipping company. It is the technical efficiency of the marine terminal operation that ensures whether the ship spends the majority of its working life in profitable employment. The design and management of the port system is a vital factor in the success or failure of the whole container concept. No matter how efficient the ship and the inland transport systems, if the terminal imposes delays through lack of investment, poor design and bad management, all gains in productivity in other parts of the overall transport system can easily be lost.

The most important advantage of containerisation, is the reduction in total time taken to transport goods from manufacturer to consumer: which can save the manufacturer other costs inherent in the order cycle for goods from the customer — that is the lead time from order placing to delivery. To speed delivery, most manufacturers must store their products close to the market. But the speed of the transport mode has an effect on the amount of stock held in warehouses in order to make guaranteed deliveries. The time saving in delivery time is accomplished by containerisation by reason of the shorter transfer time needed when moving the goods between modes. The actual time saving is dependent on the installation and use of properly designed handling equipment throughout the chain. It follows that if less time is taken in handling the actual goods and the proper packaging is used, minimal loss, damage or pilferage takes place. Traditionally, it is during the handling process both in the port terminal and elsewhere in the chain that the greatest losses occur. Although the container has minimised these risks, there is the added danger that all the contents may be stolen by having the whole box taken.

With conventional break bulk cargo handling methods, high costs are involved in packaging goods to prevent damage in transit as well as the large amount of documentation and high insurance premiums. Containerisation has brought benefits by lowering these costs but the reduction has not realised the first claims of the pioneers of the system.

Finally, handling containers in marine terminals leads to lower labour costs and higher labour morale. The lower costs are due partly to the reduction in manpower needed to handle the same throughput across a container berth as compared to a conventional berth. The labour morale of those working is higher because of the better working conditions that can be provided: the stevedore works in relatively clean and warm conditions and never has to manhandle the cargo. There has, of course, been considerable publicity on worldwide stevedore unrest at the introduction of container services, but this unrest must be viewed against a background of past employer/employee relations and understandable fears for job security rather than the improved working conditions that the introduction of containers made possible.

## Disadvantages of Containerisation

Obviously, there are some major disadvantages attached to the container system although to listen to people engaged in container operations, this fact is not too apparent. Later in this chapter the complexity of the overall organization and management of the system will be discussed. The container system sets out to give a door to door service which involves more complex control mechanisms, especially in keeping a record of where the individual containers have been sent.

To initiate a system, a great deal of very sophisticated handling equipment must be provided. This calls for a large amount of finance for investment for both the equipment itself and for training programmes for skilled people to operate it.

To earn the required returns on such high levels of capital investment, intensive use is a necessity and intensive use implies complex organization of the whole system to ensure that the throughput of containers is sufficiently high to warrant the expenditure.

One fact that seems to be common to dock workers the world over, is the willingness with which they withdraw their labour in support of other groups of dock workers or to further a particular grievance. Solidarity among dock workers has been the cry for over a century and if any capital intensive, highly integrated system is prevented from operation, there will be substantial losses incurred by the companies concerned. Containerisation has reduced the number of workers involved, but has in many cases increased the power of this reduced work force. A small number of workers in strategic positions can halt the whole operation.

There is still a great deal of cargo that cannot be containerised and on routes where containers have taken a major share, this non-containerisable cargo can be subjected to delays because the conventional service must of necessity be less frequent. This could mean higher conventional liner freight rates, although there is no real evidence of this at the moment.

## Management of the System

The idea of putting cargo into containers for carriage is not a recent one; containers in one form or another have been used to carry cargo since the early years of this century. The through transport concept is new and involves the organization and management of the whole transport chain being undertaken by a single company regardless of how many modes of transport are used. Thus control of the movement is definite rather than diverse.

For the system to be a complete success, it is essential that all operators of transport modes involved agree on a standard size of container. This standard size has to consider the limitations in size imposed by allowable measurements of the various transport vehicles; in the majority of countries these relate to the permitted dimensions of the road truck. It is the size of the road truck that sets the maximum limits on container size. There are two standard I.S.O. containers, the first 8 ft high by 8 ft wide, the second 8 ft 6 inches high and 8 ft wide, both coming in lengths of 20, 30 or 40 ft although a majority of containers used in sea transport are of 40 ft length (see Figure 3.1).

The ship has always been but one link in the distribution network from producer to consumer and before the advent of containers, the shipping company tended to divorce its activity from the other parts of that network — shipping management was only interested in the cargo after it had crossed the ship's rail. The shipping company can no longer limit its interest in this way as the financial investment in the ship and associated containers means that full utilisation must be achieved if returns on investment are to be realised. Shipping managements have now to involve themselves in all stages of the transport chain from origin to destination.

Never before has the shipowner had to consider the cargo packaging as an integral part of the ship when planning new services and further investment. As inland transport operators have neither the

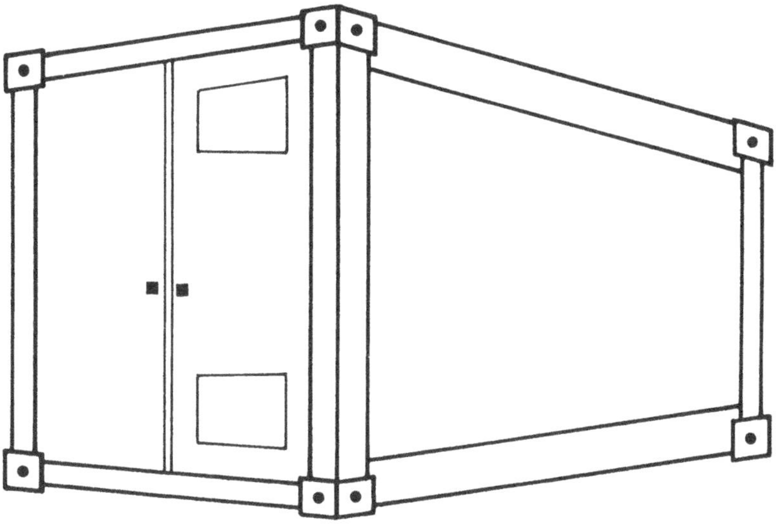

FIGURE 3.1. Standard I.S.O. container

money nor the desire to invest in containers, it has been left to the shipping companies to supply the bulk of the finance themselves. When it is realized that each ship requires at least three times the containers as the ship's capacity, the extent of the extra investment needed by the shipping company is obvious.

The last point is logical when viewed from angles other than that of investment. The ship is the link between two, often sovereign state, inland transport networks and can carry many more containers per vehicle than is possible by any other mode. This poses the question of control over the movement of the containers and the need to return each to its origin. If the inland transport operator in each country were to set up a system to monitor the movements of their own containers, the expense would be large and although the system would be easy to establish in the home base country, would require a large organization or network of agents abroad. The shipping company must, through necessity, maintain representatives in most countries and is therefore already able to set up a system of control.

Movement control is vital if the containers are to be used to their full potential. This entails, as far as possible, keeping the container full of cargo and moving through the system. A container filled with cargo but sitting in a transport terminal waiting to be unloaded, or sitting empty waiting to be transported, is wasting money for the company unless adequate waiting time payments are charged. This form of control and utilisation can only be undertaken by the shipping company through their organization at each end of the route. The shipping company can gain this degree of control by owning road haulage and railways companies and opening inland container depots for consolidating small parcels into full container loads and other forms of integration.

It is significant that the first real integrated container service was started by a road haulage company in the U.S.A. called the Maclean Trucking Company. That experimental beginning has grown into the Sea Land container service with a policy of ownership of all the equipment used in the transport of containers including port terminal equipment, trucking companies, ships and containers. By this method, they are able to plan, organize and control the total movement of their containers from far inland at one end of the route to the far inland at the other.

C.P. Ships (the container company in the Canadian Pacific organization) also run a fully integrated system. One document and one charge covers the whole movement of the container from inland Canada to its final destination. The container is taken by Canadian Pacific Railway to Wolfs Cove, loaded onto a Canadian Pacific ship by wholly owned equipment and transported across the Atlantic.

Individual European Shipping companies have found that the investment needed to establish a container service is too great a strain on their finances to overcome this problem and they have formed consortia to run the services. Each company provides part of the required investment to set up the service and shares in any profits earned from it.

The ideal container service is one where the full container is loaded onto a road or rail vehicle at the consignees premises and transported to the port and loaded onto the ship without touching the cargo inside. At the end of the sea leg, the full container is delivered to the consignor once more without touching the contents. In this way, it is only the container that has been handled once it has entered the system and this can be accomplished by mechanical equipment with a small but highly trained work force. This increases productivity and reduces the cost per tonne of cargo carried which should in turn lead to lower freight rates.

Unfortunately, there are many shippers who do not export enough at one time to fill a container and opportunity must be given for these small loads to be consolidated into full container loads. The ideal solution is to consolidate the Less than Container Load (L.C.L.) traffic into Full Container Loads (F.C.L.) as soon as possible within the transport chain and this can be accomplished at inland container depots run either by a shipping company or a freight forwarding agent.

## Container Ships

A container ship is illustrated in Figure 3.2. Although the first generation vessels were converted conventional ships, this type of ship is specifically designed to carry containers. All the early ships were independent units in that they had their own lifting gear for handling containers and could therefore use any berth that was available.

The ships now are completely cellular, their holds fitted with container guides that split the cargo space. The containers are loaded into the cells and positioned by the guides, one on top of the other so that they are held rigidly in position against the motion of the ship. Deck space is utilised by carrying containers up to four high, held in position by a combination of twist locking devices and lashings. By using the deck, approximately 30% more cargo can be carried on the average container ship than if only the holds of the ship were used. Utilising this space also compensates for the loss of cargo carrying capacity taken up by the strength members of the ship's structure and between the container cells.

However, there are problems with carrying containers on deck in such numbers, not the least of which is the stability of the ship. The weight and contents of a container must be known before it is loaded in order that the weight distribution of the cargo around the ship can be calculated on sailing. With this knowledge, the stability of the ship can be checked and if insufficient, the loading order of the containers changed. The containers are tested for racking, lifting and stacking strength and for watertightness. No matter how carefully the con-

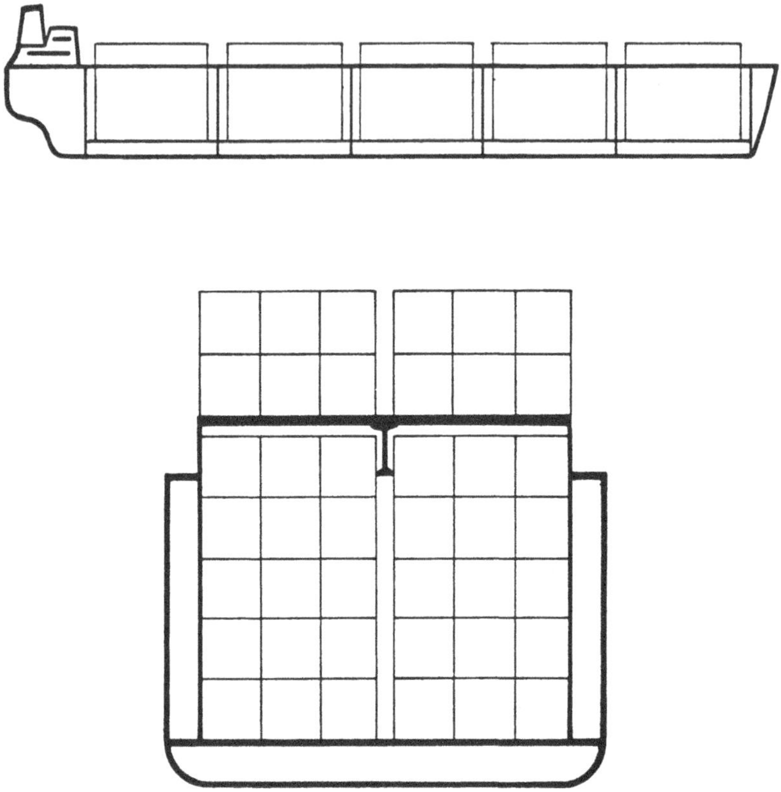

FIGURE 3.2. Container ship

tainers are handled, over time they are subject to leakage when seas are breaking over the deck due to small distortions in shape and perished gaskets around the doors. To combat leakage, it is always best policy to stow containers on deck with doors facing aft, thus keeping the opening out of the direct line of spray. Only adherence to strict inspection procedures, to be followed before the container is loaded with cargo, will risks inherent in damaged containers be minimised.

There must be some form of automatic list correcting system designed into the ship to enable the officers to keep the vessel upright when loading and discharging containers and so provide a stable environment for the containers to slide into the cell guides. Many ships have stabilisers to reduce rolling at sea to cut the stresses imposed on the containers and their contents.

The productivity of a container ship is about five to seven times greater than that of the conventional general cargo ship it is designed to replace. The productivity gains are accomplished by the ships being larger, faster, having a much quicker turn round time in port and are operated by up to 30% less crew members. They have many effects on the shipping industry, the major one being the need for far less ships to carry the same cargo volume on a given route. There has, therefore, been a need to phase out large numbers of conventional ships with the attendant danger of redundancies among crews.

## Discharge/Loading

The first generation container ships had their own cargo handling gear but it is now generally accepted practice in the deep sea trades for the ship to rely on the ports to provide the means of transfer between ship and shore.

On arrival at the berth, the deck load of containers is discharged and ferried to the import stacking area. Once this deck load is removed, one complete underdeck cell is discharged, from thereon the discharge and loading can be undertaken simultaneously. The crane alternately discharges a container from one cell and then places an export container into the next cell which has already been discharged. This means that the crane hook is fully utilised throughout its planned and its theoretical cycle.

In a publication from the Marine Transport Centre, Liverpool University, entitled "Containers and their competitors" by E.T. Lang, the most efficient handling rates are about 500 to 600 containers per day per crane. It is usual for container berths to provide two cranes per ship and to work twenty four hours a day.

The efficiency of the loading/discharge operation does not hinge solely on crane usage. It depends to a large extent on physical and managerial organization within the port terminal. We have already seen that many of the advantages of containerisation stem from the quicker turn round time of the ship in port. This turn round is achieved by utilising the greater productivity possible at a container berth as compared to that of a conventional general cargo berth and it seems to be evident that port management/labour relations are improving with the introduction of the better working conditions associated with container handling.

## The Port Terminal

The port terminal is such a crucial component of the system, that its planning within the transport chain must incorporate methods that enable it to take full advantage of the container concept; especially that containers can be speedily transferred between road, rail and sea vehicles. The location is crucial as there must be excellent access to the inland transport network increasing the size of the ports hinterland and reasonably close to the major shipping routes.

The layout of the main parts of the terminal must reflect this careful planning by ensuring the free flow of containers by avoiding, as far as possible, bottlenecks and holding points. The main components are: the berth, the transfer cranes, the container marshalling area, the container stuffing shed for Less than Container Loads, container repair area, equipment store and maintenance facilities, truck reception area, weighbridges and terminal control centre.

Container berths are usually of the marginal quay type rather than a pier in order to give greater accessibility to the land area behind them. This is very important to the operation of the terminal as careful planning can avoid the bottlenecks which invariably occur at the shore end of the pier. It is generally felt by most experts that at least 20 acres of land are needed for servicing each berth.

When the first ships were converted to carry containers, they were fitted with gantry cranes to handle the cargo. It is now generally accepted practice that the ships serving long, deep sea routes will be built without handling equipment. There are a number of reasons both economic and technical for this development. Firstly, ships cranes are very vulnerable to salt water damage and vibration problems when the ship is at sea and are very costly to maintain. To design a crane that will overcome all these problems would be very costly and saddle the shipowner with higher capital costs. Secondly, there should be greater utilisation with shore based cranes in contrast to ships cranes as the crane on the ship can only be utilised when that ship is in port, whereas the shore crane can serve a succession of ships. This emphasizes the need on the part of the shipowner for efficient cargo handling equipment to be provided at each end of the voyage.

Containers are sorted and stored in the marshalling or stacking area while awaiting transfer to the next mode of transport; either export to the ship or import to inland transport. The size of the stacking areas (one for import containers, one for export containers) will depend on the stacking method employed, the availability of land, the berth throughput and the efficiency of the inland transport collection and distribution system.

The two main methods of marshalling the containers in the stacking areas are, (1) to place each individual container on its own trailer giving accessibility and ease of movement simply by a yard tractive unit to the container and (2) stacking containers on the ground (usually two high, but where land is scarce, up to five high). The second method is far less flexible than the first.

The placement of containers should be carefully planned: if not, considerable work will be necessary merely to get handling equipment to the required item. Unproductive movement is very costly in time and equipment usage as straddle carriers need to be employed on a task outwith their usual one; that of transferring the containers from the marshalling area to the ship's side.

Most container terminals must, reluctantly, provide a transit shed for consolidating small parcels of cargo into container size loads. As mentioned earlier, consolidation, close to the source of the cargo, is not always easy to accomplish. The transit shed must be kept well away from the berth area so that the flow of containers is unimpeded. The design of the shed should allow lorry loads to be transferred straight into the containers by means of tailgate high platforms; obviously there must be a method of handling refridgerated containers.

Finally, there remains the problem of rail access to the terminal. Despite several research efforts, it has proved impossible to design a berth for unloading rail wagons directly into the ship without interrupting the flow of containers and drastically reducing the handling rate. It is, therefore, usual to site the rail connection on the edge of the terminal area, transferring the containers to the stack by straddle carrier or trailer.

Three other factors must be considered, especially when considering the future of containerisation.

## Economies of Scale

It has already been shown that economies of scale in general cargo shipping are limited by the time the ship spends in port loading and discharging and that the inability of operators to increase handling rates faster than increases in ship size generally means longer in port on a pro rata basis. The report "Containers and their competitors" points out that container ship size increases compared to those of the conventional general cargo ships they replaced are limited in the same way: once the ship has reached a certain size, the period spent in port starts to take up an increasing proportion of operating time especially if size increases are accompanied by speed increases in journey time. The result: costs rise to a point where any saving in the costs of the sea leg by bigger ships are offset by increases in port costs. Physical limits on increased size are also set by port constraints and canal dimensions. Economies of scale can be gained by increasing the size of the container and greater utilisation of berth space and cranes. Nevertheless, the report tends to state that productivity gains from economies of scale will be very small in the future.

## Feeder Services

It is generally accepted that the future deep sea transport of containers will involve the use of large container ships calling at a limited number of ports at each end of the voyage. This leads to the conclusion that a network of minor feeding routes plied by smaller container vessels will be needed to service the large, deep sea ports.

## The Landbridge Concept

There is now concrete evidence that the land bridge principle is a major source of competition to the longer container routes. The theory underlying this concept is, that to enable the container to travel along the shortest route between two places, the container is shipped between continents, transhipped to rail for transport across the continent and loaded aboard ship if necessary for a final sea crossing. Obviously, there are a number of routes where this principle could be utilised but the two outstanding examples are both on trade routes between Europe and Japan: one uses Canadian or U.S. railways, the other uses the Trans Siberian Railway through the Soviet Union. The service must bear the added cost of transhipment between sea and rail but the container system enhances the transfer process by making savings in time and by bulk use of the rail system can offset the extra costs of transhipment. Shipping companies operating container vessels must be aware of sources of competition and design their service accordingly.

## Major Effects of Containerisation

The major effects that containerisation of general cargo has had on the shipping industry can be identified within five broad areas.

- Heavy capital investment is necessary in ships, containers and port handling equipment to maximise the use of the system and capitalise on its undoubted advantages. This type of investment calls for detailed and careful planning of both the technological system and the management administration regime if adequate returns are to be earned.
- To achieve a high level of return, and indeed generate the necessary investment funds, the external relationships of shipping organizations have undergone radical change. The setting up of consortia of shipowners to run container services, often across national boundaries, have made container shipping companies much more co-operative.
- The internal organization and attitude of the shipping company personnel has changed as it is no longer possible to sit back and just sell ship space. The complete container service must be sold to the customer to utilise the container fully and this involves shipping company personnel in the conduct of total transport of goods from manufacturer to consumer.
- The shipping company must have a detailed knowledge of what

is arriving at the port so that the ship can be loaded quickly and without delay while the cargo is checked. It is important to know the weight, contents and destination of each container so that the loading plan can be calculated before the ship arrives, thus minimising port time.

- One claim for containerisation has always been that it should lead to a simplification of the tariff structure. There is a lot of evidence that simplification is taking place although it is generally felt that this is as a result of competition from other modes of transport than a direct desire on the part of shipping companies to lower their rate structure. The development of freight of all kinds (F.A.K.) rates on some short sea routes bears out the last point. Here, competitive modes are non-commodity discriminatory in their charging policy but charge a box rate.

The claim that containerisation would bring stability to the rate structure has not materialised in practice, although it is claimed that as services have improved in quality and speed, rate increases have in fact been slowed by the introduction of the system.

Containerisation has had a profound effect on the shipping industry as a result of the introduction of new technologies and in the changed management organization. The question now to be asked is whether containerisation is the ultimate means of transporting manufactured goods or whether or not the other unit load systems have a part to play. The next chapter deals with the question.

## FURTHER READING

Gilman, S., *Ship choice in the Container Age*, Cargo Systems Publication, New Malden, Surrey, 1980.

Gilman, S., R. Maggs, and S. Ryder, *Containers on the North Atlantic*, Marine Transport Centre, University of Liverpool, Liverpool, 1980.

Laing, E.J., *Containers and Their Competitors*, Marine Transport Centre, University of Liverpool, Liverpool, 1978.

N.P.C., *Transhipment in the Seventies*, National Ports Council, London, 1969.

Van Den Burg, G., *Containerisation and Other Unit Load Systems*, Hutchinson Benham, London, 1974.

Whittiker, J.R., *Containerisation*, Transcripta Books, London, 1974.

# 4 Other Unit Load Systems

The motivation and drive behind the development of technical innovations by the shipping industry is derived from the constant search for methods of operation which will reduce or at least stabilise the rapid escalation in costs associated with traditional practices. This is especially true when considering liner shipping where, until very recently, labour costs accounted for a significant proportion of total operating costs.

The major innovation has been the development of containerisation as described in Chapter 3. As more and more routes are containerised either fully or partially, the system has come to be regarded as the answer to the problems besetting general cargo shipping.

There are, however, a number of disadvantages attached to containerisation which have generated a great deal of research into, and development of, other methods of handling and carriage that fulfil the basic aims of unit load systems, namely: quick handling in port, intermodality and greater productivity from the cargo carrying units. Containerisation of any trade route involves the shipping and transport industries in planning and building a complete network exclusively for the handling of standard sized units which calls for a large injection of finance to buy ships, build port facilities, supply containers and re-train the existing workforce. The equipment must be intensively used in order to earn sufficient returns to repay capital expenditure, if economic benefits are to be realised. This demands complex organizational structures and a willingness on the part of those involved to replace traditional working practices by more flexible ones. On many routes there remains a significant amount of cargo that cannot be fitted into a standard container. This freight can be subject to delays as conventional cargo liner services become less frequent and more expensive.

The container system requires that shipowners, port operators and inland transport companies accept that the infrastructure be designed to cater for a particular type of cargo packaging. A minority view, held by some port planners and shipowners, is that there is a need to design and build shipping systems that can operate into existing ports, rather than involve the port managements in making large investments in specialised equipment at a few berths, which may in the long run cause problems with redundant but not life expired conventional berths. This is especially true when considering the improvement in shipping services from developed to developing countries. It is not surprising that the shipowner from a developed country wishes to utilise his heavy investment in that country and is prepared to tolerate a less than perfect system in the developing country. There is also the question of delay and cost of port development in countries which are at the same time using materials and funds to build up other sectors of their infrastructure.

As has been stated before, all unit load systems have the same aims: they are developed to minimise time spent in port, benefit from economies of scale and utilise standard materials handling equipment. The systems generally thought to compete with containerisation have the advantage that they can be used at both modern and antiquated berths and do not demand sophisticated equipment.

## Palletisation

A pallet is defined as "a flat, portable platform constructed to sustain the load and to permit handling by mechanical equipment".

Pallets are extensively used in worldwide distribution and are relatively inexpensive. They consist of a flat platform supported on bearers wide enough apart to allow the forks of a lift truck to be placed underneath.

The pallet was first used in the shipping industry as a means of speeding the loading and discharge of conventional ships, the cargo being secured to the pallet either in the transit shed or at the shipper's premises. This practice caused problems at many ports as government regulations laid down the type of pallet to be used by dockers and the tests that they had to undergo. It would be an impossible task to certify every pallet in use in the world's distribution system and port labour was reluctant to have an untested pallet hanging over their heads suspended from a crane. When these problems were overcome, usually by loading the shipper's pallet on top of a standard docks pallet, it was possible to use fork lift trucks in the holds of ships to speed up the cargo handling process.

As the pallet is designed to be handled by fork lift trucks, the greatest efficiency will result if this capacity can be utilised at all times. To accomplish this, all movement of cargo must be horizontal, cutting out the vertical lifts by crane. The pallet is designed to allow this type of movement.

The ship has side ports in the hull at quay level and ramps or elevators to lift the pallets between decks in the ship. All decks are completely flat to facilitate ease of movement of fork lift trucks and the hold are connected by watertight doors to allow a free run over the length of the ship. There are wide weather tight hatches on the upper deck to allow the loading of large non-palletised cargo which can be a problem on many routes.

The system fits in very well with both conventional port facilities and the rest of the transport and distribution network. In its most favourable mode, the cargo is loaded on and fixed securely to the pallet at the factory and transported to the port by lorry or rail. At the port, the pallet loads are assembled into ship capacity and destination loads in a transit shed and then loaded onto the ship by fork lift trucks. The transfer from shore to ship is via the side doors and between decks by elevators. At all stages of the operation, the cargo remains strapped to the pallet whilst it is handled by fork lift truck (see Figure 4.1). Even if it is not possible to have all the cargo palletised at the factory, it is relatively easy to feed cargo into the flow at any point in the system, for instance at a freight forwarder's warehouse or even the transit shed.

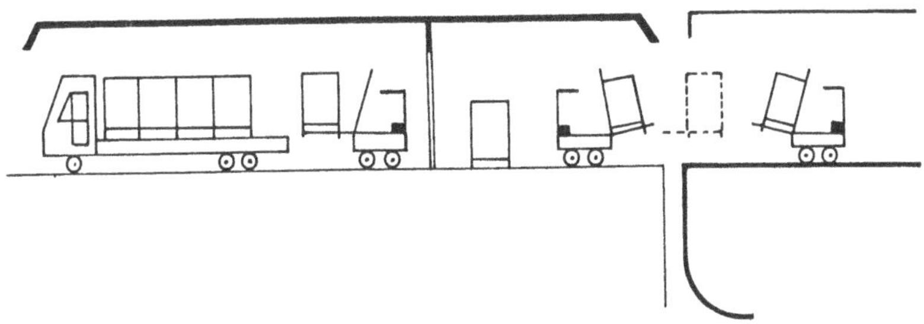

FIGURE 4.1. Pallet ship loading operation

Palletisation is relatively inexpensive, achieves substantial savings in time spent in port and on manpower and uses equipment and expertise that has been widespread in distribution for many decades. It suffers from the disadvantage that the unit is not weatherproof and needs covered storage in the port. Additionally, work must stop during rain. The cheapness and simplicity of the pallet has led many people within the shipping industry to question why it has not been used to a greater extent. In the 1960's, when shipowners were looking for ways to solve the escalating problem of rising costs, some U.S. owners plumped for containerisation and the rest of the world followed. Perhaps the simplicity and cheapness of the pallet was overlooked in the process.

## Roll on Roll off

With every other transport mode it is possible to load the vehicles from the side, front, rear and top; ships have traditionally been loaded exclusively from the top through relatively small hatches.

The Roll on Roll off technique has been used for waterborne transport for a considerable time, especially with river crossing and train ferries. The system came into general use during the affluent period following World War II as surplus tank landing craft were used by enterprising businessmen to ferry freight lorries and passenger accompanied cars across narrow strips of water separating two countries, such as the English Channel.

The underlying concept of the Roll on Roll off system is the use of a movable bridge, the cargo being driven on and off under its own power. As a means of transporting general cargo and passenger cars over short distances, Roll on Roll off means a great deal of time saving; lorries and cars are driven on and off the ship by their drivers and port turn-round is kept to a minimum. On many routes, the sea passage can be used by the driver of a commercial vehicle as part of the statutory rest time laid down by government legislation.

Roll on Roll off in its pure form becomes less economic as distance increases as the driver and tractive unit is under-utilised and the cost penalty of having assets tied up is prohibitive for the road haulage company. There is also uneconomic use of space around the underside of lorry trailers. On short voyages this wasted capacity is compensated for by the quickness of turn-round in port. Hence, although a greater number of voyages are achieved over a given time period turn-round time is less significant over longer journeys.

The Roll on Roll off system tends to be fairly flexible in the type of cargo that can be carried — from large indivisible loads to containers on trailers. The main advantage of the system is that there is no need for sophisticated cargo handling equipment in port, thus reducing the need for investment. However, a large area of land needs to be available for parking lorries and trailers while they await loading.

### The Ships

The main cargo handling component of the ship is a ramp which connects the main vehicle deck to the shore, usually at the stern of the vessel. In those parts of the world where the tidal range is high, the port must provide some form of "link span" bridge which acts as a levelling device, moving up and down with the tide on a hinge attached to the shore. This solves the problem of ship/berth height.

The ships tend to be very versatile and can be discharged using very small areas of quay by mooring stern to the warf. There have been developments in ramp design to take advantage of this versatility by fitting angled ramps which enable the ship to tie up parallel to the quay and use the ramp at the stern while discharging cargo from forward via side ports. Very modern ships have ramps that can be slewed from right astern to other angles so that the ship can fit into any berthing configuration (Figure 4.2).

The vessels can be categorised into four main groups.

- Passenger/vehicle ferries are predominantly employed on short-voyages across narrow straits separating two states and are designed to cater mainly for business and leisure traffic consisting of passenger accompanied cars. Apart from the vehicle decks, they have all the functions of major passenger liners. They have ramps at both the bow and the stern to ensure shorter turn-round times by using the drive on drive straight off principle, i.e. through the bow at one end, the stern at the other. There is generally sufficient height on the main deck to carry some commercial vehicles which adds to their profit potential, especially at off peak times.

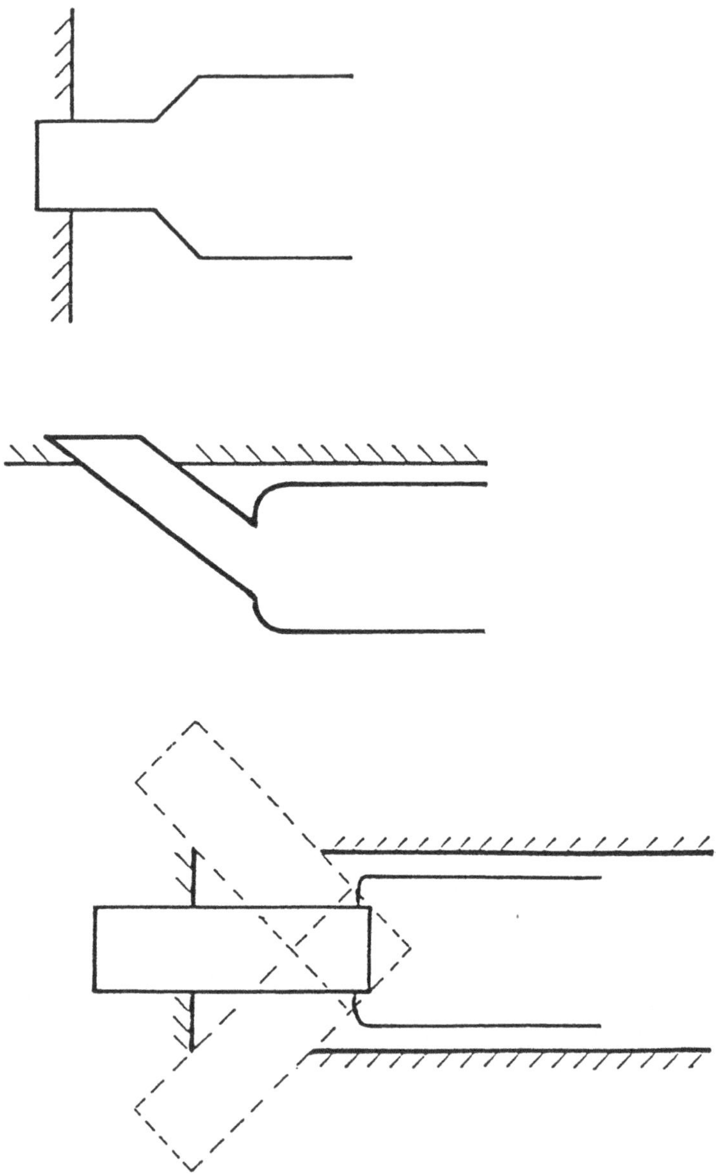

FIGURE 4.2. Roll on roll off ramp configurations

• Short sea cargo ferries are designed exclusively for carrying road haulage traffic and are made more efficient by encorporating the ramps, elevators and deck heights needed to handle the expected lorry weights and sizes. Generally, accommodation for drivers accompanying trucks is sparse and the financial costs involved in providing stronger decks and wider passageways is not necessarily offset by any advantage from faster journey time.

• Deep Sea Roll on Roll off ships have built up an increasingly good reputation in ports with a lack of container handling equipment. The cargo is loaded onto trailers and pulled into the ship by a tractor, either carried on board ship or supplied by the port authority. Any cargo can be carried as long as the ramp size and strength is adequate for the weights involved and there is sufficient cubic space in the holds. This ability is very valuable when a trade route is opened up to a rapidly developing country, like those in the Middle East, where a fair proportion of cargo is developed material and not easily containerisable. On established routes between two developed countries, the ships are hybrids with a mixture of cellular space for containers and Ro Ro space for non-containerisable cargo such as large indivisible loads for trailers and fully finished cars.

• There has been and continues to be a steady increase in the trade in ready for market cars, the largest exporter being the Japanese. At one time ready assembled vehicles were carried in bulk carriers on portable lightweight decks that could be stowed away when the ship was used to carry bulk cargo. Indeed this greatly increased the utilisation of these ships. Specifically designed car carrying ships have, however, been designed for these trades — with side and stern doors, internal ramps between decks and a characteristic shape with very high sides which gives them the appearance of having too much freeboard. The reason for this shape is that cars stow at 700 and by building decks into the superstructure, and using deck space, more freight can be carried thereby compensating for the broken stowage below decks.

## Port Congestion

There is considerable accumulated research to support the view that ports in developing countries are thoroughly inefficient and that, despite the provision of some sophisticated facilities, the throughputs at most berths are relatively small when compared with those in developed countries. This poor performance is due to a number of factors chief of which are poor administration, poor organization and a lack of investment in shore based facilities.

If inefficiency is combined with haphazard forward planning, severe congestion in the port area can result. U.N.C.T.A.D. (The United Nations Commission on Trade and Development) has estimated that in a bad year, such as 1976, the world cost of port congestion was $5000 million, if interest on capital tied up in ships and cargo is taken into account. The reports argue that congestion not only causes losses to the shipping industry, but adds to world inflation rates.

It is, however, a very difficult task to forecast the demand for capacity in a developing country and port authorities in those countries are left with a choice; either they invest in facilities which may give the capacity to handle projected future traffic with the danger that the traffic may not materialise or they invest at a much lower level and face the possibility of congestion. It must always be remembered that it is not just financial criteria that are used in making a choice as unquantifiable factors such as national pride have a part to play.

One factor that has caused an increased interest to be shown in Roll on Roll off tonnage is the effect of port congestion on vital imports to an economy. There was an upsurge of trade between developed nations and the oil exporting countries in the mid-nineteen seventies, fuelled by the extra revenue from oil sales; however, many of the ports in these countries had lacked investment and were unable to cope with the sudden rise in traffic. In other parts of the world, the ports relied on handling methods that were very labour intensive — a politically sound policy in the circumstances — but when import volumes rose, the labour force and handling methods became overstretched and unable to cope. Lack of investment combined with a lack of planning, left many ports with insufficient storage in the port area and poor inland transport links proved inadequate for the volumes of traffic they were meant to handle. All these factors taken together resulted in long port delays for many ships and in addition to already rising shipping costs forced the conference lines to impose freight surcharges for going to heavily congested ports. These surcharges brought forth accusations of discrimination from the developing countries' shipping industries as they were seen to apply unfairly in a situation over which the port management had very little control.

The Roll on Roll off shipping system has certain advantages which help to combat both port congestion and the need to build up the port infrastructure before large volumes of imports can be handled. Containerisation needs sophisticated equipment and a port management organization trained to operate the system and involves not only large financial investment but a significant period of time in which to build the facilities and train the personnel. Roll on Roll off methods overcome these problems by requiring only a basic berth on which to land the ramp and, by tying up stern first, cut down on the amount of berth space each ship needs. The handling rates for loading and discharge are up to five times higher than conventional methods and the ships can transport a wider range of cargo than container ships thus providing a service that fits the imports associated with an economic growth pattern for a developing country.

## Barge Carrying Vessels

It is suggested by research undertaken by colleagues and myself at Loughborough University that the problem of port congestion is compounded by the need to design and construct deep water berths and associated facilities which demand time and finance. Under these conditions there seems a need for a shipping technology which reduces the need for sophisticated berth facilities, or eliminates this need altogether, while at the same time is flexible enough to be able to respond to any change in the type of service demanded and to give the shipowner a quick turn-round in port.

To accomplish this, there is a need to separate the two functions of sea transport and materials handling as with almost all shipping methods these are combined in such a way that at different stages of the voyage one or the other is redundant. There is limited need for the motive power that drives the ship at sea when that ship is in port, or for the materials handling equipment when that ship is at sea. The methods of unitisation already described, efficient as they are in terms of turn-round times, do not affect this separation. The container or Roll on Roll off vessel is still all too dependent on non-predictable port conditions. Thus, it can be argued that the container or Roll on Roll off ship is not a solution to what many would accept as the fundamental problem; the ship in port. Where the container system is used in an advanced economy, with all the potential for port planning and construction, relatively easy financial arrangements and personnel training opportunities, there is no doubt that the system is both efficient and economic.

While no ultimate solution to the ship in port problem is possible within the foreseeable future, the idea to separate the deep sea transportation function from the port cargo handling function is most apparent in the barge carrier and comes closest to the ideal. It is a simple concept but involves the use of complex technology to overcome practical difficulties. Like the container system it is the result of American research and development which has stemmed from the need for greater productivity in the United States registered shipping fleet.

As has already been stated, the barge carrier system separates the functions of sea transport and materials handling. The barge carrying vessel is merely a vehicle for carrying cargo on a proportion of the total journey from the producer to consumer. It is designed to transport full barges from the seaward end of one inland waterway system to the seaward end of another. The system is made up of three components, the barge carrying vessel (generally termed the mother ship), the barges designed to be towed along the inland waterway system in groups and the system for transferring the barges from and to the sea.

The underlying philosophy of the concept is that the cost of the transport system as a whole can be kept to a minimum if the component representing the largest investment, (the ship) is fully utilised. Therefore, the methods of operation must seek to keep the ship moving as much as possible to achieve full potential. Unloading cargo must be undertaken at a different place and time to that spent by the ship in port. To accomplish this, the barges are loaded at an inland port or at a waterside berth adjacent to the shipper's premises, towed in blocks to sheltered waters by tug and loaded onto the ship. The ship then sails on the sea leg and, on arrival at the end of the sea passage, the barges are discharged and distributed through the inland waterway system. As soon as the barges have left the ship, a preloaded set of barges are taken on board and the ship sails. At no time, from one inland loading point to another inland discharge point, is the cargo in the barges handled. If the transfer time for loading/discharging the ship is faster than other methods, port costs can be reduced.

The only facility that the barge carrying vessel needs in order to operate successfully is an adequate depth of sheltered water and sufficient room to turn the ship and marshal the barges. The cargo is stowed in relatively shallow draft barges that can be discharged/loaded at a variety of unsophisticated lighterage berths with limited water depth. This system bypasses the need for costly deep water berths for handling ocean going ships and does not require advanced cargo handling gear.

It is hardly surprising that the idea was developed in the U.S.A. which has a vast heavily used system of navigable rivers and waterways. Research has shown that a system that would permit onward movement of already loaded barges, from the inland waterway network to the open sea, without the need for cargo transhipment, had obvious potential cost savings.

The efficiency of the system relies on the reliability of the equipment used to load and discharge the barges from the mother ship. There are three methods currently used to load barges: gantry crane, immersible elevator or floating barges into the ship.

The gantry crane runs on rails the length of the weather deck, behind the superstructure which is placed well forward, (see Figure 4.3) and out over a cantilever structure at the stern, allowing a clear lift and providing a docking area for the barges before being lifted. The whole operation is dependent on the efficiency of this crane; there is no other means of loading/discharging barges. A breakdown will leave the ship stranded in port and could cause major delays. The crane which has to lift almost 500 tonnes at a time, needs a constant tensioning device to overcome the problem of a slack hoist wire becoming suddenly tight as the barge moves up and down in the waves. The theoretical productivity of the crane is about four lifts an hour, which, with a payload of about 350 tonnes per barge, gives throughput of 1,400 tonnes per hour for this type of ship. The productivity obtained from the crane is affected by the sea conditions, the amount of travel along the deck and the mechanical condition of the crane; in practice it has been found to be less than the four lifts an

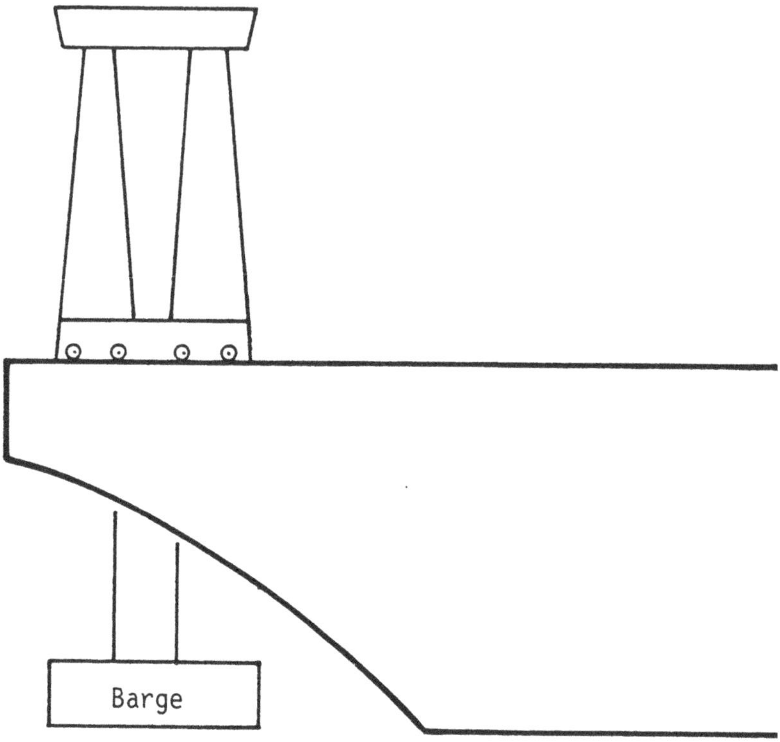


FIGURE 4.3. Gantry crane barge lift system

hour designed into the system.

The immersible lift method has a submerged elevator at the stern which allows barges or sets of barges to float over it before being lifted. On the Seabee system, two barges can be hoisted at one time which represents a lift of about 1,900 tonnes. The barges are then manoeuvred into the stowage position by hydraulic ramps and wire tackles. Once again this system is dependent on the condition of the elevator; a complete failure would leave the ship without a means of loading or discharging the barges.

The 'float on float off' works on the same principle as a floating dry dock in that the vessel is ballasted low in the water and the barges are floated into the hold via stern or bow doors. The ballast is discharged leaving the barges to be lashed for the sea voyage in a dry hold.

**Barge Carriers and Developing Countries**

As with most technical innovation which has taken place in shipping, the motivation behind the evolution and development of the barge carrying system resulted from the constant search for methods and techniques which would offset the rapidly rising costs of operating conventional ships, with a desire to utilise existing port facilities. It is highly significant that the barge carrier was first used on trade routes between developed countries with extensive waterway systems but in competition with other technologically advanced methods taking advantage of the inland transport systems. The real potential of the barge carrier may have been overlooked in this environment.

The use of barge carriers is increasing on many routes between developed and developing countries. There are several factors that make the barge carrier an appropriate system for the developing countries shipping needs.

The export trades of many developing countries contain a large amount of neo-bulk and non-containerisable cargo which is normally carried in conventional general cargo ships or bulk carriers. One difficulty experienced by shippers in these countries is their inability to amass enough cargo to fill a whole vessel without the extra costs of lengthy storage periods. With a barge carrier service, the shipper can move as little as 350 tonnes at a time, cutting down on storage and helping with production planning by providing regular transport intervals.

Industrial development in many developing countries is taking place in close proximity to the ports. This draws in large volumes of imports, much of which is containerisable. On the other hand, the export cargoes are drawn from a wide area served by low quality inland transport systems; much of the cargo is not containerisable. In many cases, these export cargo generation points could easily be served by inland waterways connected to barge carriers for the deep sea voyage. The use of barges permits the utilisation of labour intensive methods of loading and discharge at shallow water berths and is far less disruptive socially as the cargo handling points are dispersed throughout the waterway system, spreading job opportunities around the country. As barge carriers do not need extensive port development, the resulting savings in finance can be used in other parts of the economy.

Containerisation necessitates large scale developments of expensive port facilities and, of necessity, the substitution of labour by capital equipment. The barge carrier, on the other hand, allows the effective use of existing facilities and methods, encourages the growth of smaller ports and can help to disperse economic activity away from congested port areas.

## Hybrid Systems

There is no doubt that on the majority of routes between ports in developed countries where a large proportion of the trade is in manufactured goods, the container system has gained a dominant position. It has involved the expenditure of large sums of money and has changed the methods of operation of all modes of transport. The container has, therefore, been physically integrated not only into sea transport but into most areas of materials handling.

On routes between developed and developing countries there is a tendency to start a container service to fit the pattern in the developed country. This involves the shipowner in dealing with inefficiencies at one end of the route in order to profit from efficiency at the other. Recent developments have tried to combine all unit systems together — container cells, Roll on Roll off and barge capacity on the same vessel.

All unit load systems attempt to increase the productivity of the general cargo carrier by changing the methods of handling individual packages in order that the system is more in line with bulk handling methods. This involves handling homogeneous cargo by mechanical means with equipment especially designed for the task. We have seen that once the handling problem is solved, shipping companies can turn their attention to the benefits of scale economies.

## FURTHER READING


Dewry, H.P., *Roll on Roll off Shipping*, Shipping Study No. 87, 1980. H.P. Dewry Shipping Publications, London.

Dewry, H.P., *The Scope for Barge Carrying Systems*, Shipping Study No. 41, 1976. H.P. Dewry Shipping Publications, London.

Fairplay, *Fairplay Guide to Roll on Roll off Shipping*, Fairplay Publications, London, 1980.

Gilman, S., G. Williams and C. Hughes, *Roll on Roll off ships for the Deep Sea Trade*, Marine Transport Centre, University of Liverpool, Liverpool, 1978.

Hilling, D., *Barge Carrier Systems. Inventory and Prospects*, Benn Publications, London, 1978.

Law, P.R., *The Roll on Roll off System*, I.C.H.C.A., London, 1980.

# 5 Dry Bulk Cargoes

A dry bulk cargo is defined as a cargo of solids or particles loaded directly into a ship's hold without protective packaging. It is the lack of packaging that distinguishes this type of cargo from general cargo and in most cases the commodity is carried in full ship loads from one shipper. In the past, these cargoes have been referred to as "tramp cargoes", a term derived from the methods of organizing that section of the industry involved in their transport. The "tramp" is conventionally constructed with a tween deck and cargo gear and seeks employment anywhere in the world, carrying any commodity at a freight rate negotiated between the shipowner and shipper. The freight rate is dependent on prevailing market conditions for its level. The ships carry bulk commodities on voyages or time charters but can be chartered by general cargo liner shipping companies to cover deficiencies in their liner fleets. Therefore, the term "tramp cargoes" is misleading, as the majority of bulk cargoes are carried in bulk carriers specifically designed for the task of moving large amounts of raw materials, over specific trade route, on which, loading and discharge facilities are designed with the ship size in mind.

The type and size of bulk carrier hired to carry any given quantity of a commodity depends on a number of factors, including the trade route, the inherent physical qualities of the commodity and the stowage factor. Before describing the design and layout of the ships and their methods of operation it is felt that a brief discussion of these factors is necessary.

## Cargo Handling Hazards

There are a number of hazards associated with the carriage of bulk cargoes and it is usual to group these under three main headings.

## Improper Weight Distribution

Unless cargo is distributed throughout the available cargo space in a logical and planned way, there is a danger of damage to the ship's structure. There are two factors involved when considering the distribution of the cargo and these must be overcome if damage is not to occur.

- There is the danger of concentrating the weight of the cargo on small areas of deck by allowing it to pile up in the hatch square. This can be overcome by trimming the cargo into the wings of the ship using a bulldozer or by moving the end of the loading shute.
- There is the danger of distributing cargo between the holds of a ship, especially with cargoes of low stowage factor, such that the ship is fully loaded to her design draft before all the cargo space is utilised. The decision as to which holds to load and which to leave empty is crucial to the safe operation of the ship. By distributing cargo the wrong way, excessive shearing forces can occur within the structure of the ship as the buoyancy and weight forces are completely unbalanced.

## Incorrect Stability

A ship's stability is a measure of its ability to return to the upright after being heeled by an external force such as the wind or a wave. The position of the centre of gravity of ship and cargo has a major bearing on stability. There are two aspects to this problem; one associated with the positioning of the cargo during loading and the other with the behaviour of the cargo during the voyage.

Incorrect stability after loading is usually caused by placing too much cargo low down in the ship's hold, lowering the centre of gravity to such an extent that the righting moment is too large, resulting in very violent rolling in rough seas. A small heel will cause a disproportionate reaction, causing the ship to return quickly to the upright and beyond. There is a danger that the structure of the ship will be damaged as a result of stress.

All bulk commodities will shift to a greater or lesser degree during a voyage either because the physical properties of the cargo make movement easy or because moisture content is too high. As the ship rolls, the cargo can shift and put strain on the structure or cause a list.

**Spontaneous Heating**

Many bulk commodities when damp, heat up spontaneously and, in extreme cases, catch fire. Spontaneous heating takes place when moisture causes a chemical reaction in the commodity.

**Stowage Factors**

The total volume of any commodity that can be carried by ship depends upon the ship's dimensions and the usable available space within it. Utilising the available space depends upon the stowage factor of the commodity — defined as the volume of one tonne of that commodity expressed in cubic metres per tonne. Each commodity has an intrinsic stowage factor, and, assuming there is no broken stowage, (that is the cargo is free to run into all parts of the hold) there is a relationship between the quantity of cargo carried and the stowage factor.

Maximum cargo carrying weight is defined as deadweight. (The term includes consumable items used on the voyage such as fuel and stores so there will be less cargo weight available with any given deadweight, the more stores and fuel are needed to complete the voyage.) The deadweight is also a product of the underwater volume of the ship when it is down to its load draft and the cargo carrying capacity of the internal volume of the holds. The ratio of hold volume to maximum cargo weight is also a characteristic of each ship and is usually expressed as a cargo stowage rate.

To take a simple example to illustrate the stowage rate, let us take a ship with a deadweight tonnage of 100,000 and an internal volume of 140,000 $m^3$. Assuming that all the deadweight tonnage is available for cargo, the ship will have a stowage rate of $1.4m^3$/tonne to load fully down to her marks. There is obviously a relationship between the stowage factor of the cargo and the stowage rate for the ship; a further three examples will suffice to illustrate this point.

• If a shipper offers 100,000 tonnes of cargo with a stowage factor of $0.5m^3$/tonne, the ship will be down to her (marks) load draft with all 100,000 tonnes of cargo loaded but only $50,000m^3$ of cargo space used. Thus only 37.5% of available space will have been utilised.

• If the shipper offers 100,000 tonnes of cargo with a stowage factor of $1.4m^3$/tonne, the ship will be down to her load draft when 100,000 tonnes of cargo is loaded and $140,000m^3$ of space utilised. This means that all the available cargo space has been filled.

• If the shipper offers 100,000 tonnes of cargo stowing at $2.1m^3$/ tonne, the ship will only have loaded 66,600 tonnes when $140,000m^3$ of space is used. She will not be at her loaded draft which means that this ship would be unable to load all the cargo on offer.

It is obvious that consideration of stowage factors is vital to the safe construction and operation of bulk carriers. There are two other characteristics that effect the design and safe operation of vessels used to carry cargoes in bulk.

## Angle of Repose

The majority of bulk commodities form a cone shaped pile when emptied onto a flat surface and allowed to run free (an experiment with washing powder, sugar and any other household product will confirm this). The angle subtended between the slope of the pile and the horizontal plane is termed the *angle of repose* and this angle is an indication of the tendency of the commodity to *flow*. Each commodity has a characteristic angle of repose and the degree of danger of the cargo shifting during the voyage is a function of this angle. The smaller the angle of repose, the greater the danger of the cargo shifting, as even a relatively small angle of heel can take the cargo slope past the angle at which the commodity starts to flow, especially during periods of bad weather. This cargo shift can affect the stability of the ship by causing the centre of gravity to rise and endanger the ship. It is recommended by I.M.O. that all commodities with an angle of repose of less than 35% require some form of levelling of the cargo surface into the wings of the hold.

## Moisture Content

*Moisture content* is the proportion of liquid within a commodity expressed as a percentage of the total weight of cargo. Before many bulk commodities are loaded onto a ship they are processed to separate some of the impurities. "Purification" is carried out by "washing" which leaves the commodity in a wet state needing drying. A "wet" cargo is liable to assume the characteristics of a liquid cargo during a sea voyage if the moisture content is too high. This poses grave dangers for a ship designed to carry dry bulk cargoes that does not have additional strength to resist the forces generated by surges of heavy liquids, (especially when compounded with the danger of the effects of free surface on ship stability). Measurement of the moisture content of any commodity is imperative and various methods have been developed to ascertain it.

I.M.O. have drawn up a code of Safe Practice for the carriage of bulk cargoes and this document should always be consulted.

## Bulk Trades

It is important in a study of the shipping industry to review the relative importance of different bulk commodities in world trade terms in order to judge the role played by bulk shipping. Dry bulk cargoes constitute about 40% of seaborne trade in dry cargoes and are by far the most significant in terms of shipping charter activity. The bulk shipping sector also accounts for a large proportion of the rapid growth of seaborne trade since the early 1950's. When expressed in terms of tonne miles, iron ore accounts for approximately 10% of all shipping movements, coal 3% and grain 4%.

A brief description of some of the major commodities and their characteristics follows, and this provides an insight into some of the technical problems that have to be solved in order to make their carriage safe and economic.

## Iron Ore

Iron Ore is the single most important dry bulk commodity with well over 90% of all ship loads being carried in bulk carriers. The iron ore trade is closely connected with the steel making industries so it follows that shipping movements in this commodity are closely controlled by the large industrial companies that control steel making capacity. Steel companies also control, or at least have an input into, the design of loading and discharge facilities so are able to match ore throughput to the needs of the plants served by these facilities. A major aim has been to take advantage of economies of scale in both ore shipment and steel production plant.

The trade in iron ore has steadily increased from 247.1 million tonnes in 1970 to 320.8 million tonnes in 1979 but the growth of the fleet has been proportionately greater. The growth in fleet size is indicative of the changing patterns of trade resulting from longer voyage lengths from sources of ore to industrial complexes. The average length of haul has risen from approximately 3950 miles in 1970 to approximately 5000 miles in 1979.

In 1970, the median size of a ship was between 40,000 and 60,000 deadweight tonnes but by the end of 1979 over 56% of the fleet engaged in the iron ore trade were over 100,000 tonnes deadweight with the majority specifically designed ore carriers.

There are very few problems associated with the carriage of iron ore especially when ore carriers are used and a few simple rules are followed. The main problem area is the distribution of the cargo between holds, especially when tween deck ships are still used.

Loading is usually by ship loaders fed by conveyor from large storage areas and the excellent flow characteristics of iron ore mean that loading rates can reach 20,000 tonnes per hour. Discharge is invariably by large clam grabs and rates of 6,000 tonnes per hour are not uncommon.

Most iron ore is processed before shipment by washing, grinding, screening and consolidation which removes some of the unwanted impurities. This process leaves a powdery substance with a high water content which can cause problems with dust during loading and discharging and high moisture content during the voyage.

## Grain

The term grain when used in the shipping industry is taken to include wheat, maize, oats, rye, barley, seeds and pulses (peas and beans). Approximately 146 million tonnes of grain was shipped during 1979 but forecasting the amount that will be carried in any one year is a very imprecise exercise as world climatic and political conditions have large effects on shipments. The sudden failure of a harvest, political embargoes, wars and world agricultural aid programmes all cause sudden surges in the demand for grain imports, impose problems for the shipping industry and alter the route patterns and the ports used. The irregular trading pattern and use of different types of port effects the type and size of the ships used as investment in port facilities depends to a large extent on the regularity of their use.

The carriage of grain causes problems for all agencies engaged in its handling due to the physical characteristics of the commodity and the control needed for storage, loading and discharge. Grain shipped wet, green or in an unseasoned condition is liable to heat up or sweat and is ruined, by the end of the voyage. At the loading port the ships holds will be inspected to ascertain whether they are clean and suitable for carrying grain and the commodity itself surveyed before and during loading to ensure that it is fit for carriage.

The main danger to all grain carrying ships is the liability of the cargo to shift during the voyage due to the small angle of repose. All grains settle during a sea passage: an apparently full hold on sailing, will have 10% space above the surface by the end of the voyage. Settlement can be reduced in ships not specifically designed to carry grain by fitting boards vertically along the centre of the holds to reduce free surface and fitting feeders in the hatches. The feeders gradually release grain into the hold and fill the space left as it settles. All ships used in the grain trade must comply with I.M.O. Grain Regulations when loading or transporting cargoes.

The nature of the commodity — free flowing granules — facilitiates the loading and discharge process. Loading is generally by overhead conveyors with covered shutes which can be moved in order to level the grain throughout the hold space. Discharge is generally by suction systems, although in places where emergency shipments are being handled very primitive methods are sometimes used.

The grain trade tends to offer opportunities for employment to all sizes and types of ship. However, in recent years there has been a strong trend towards the larger sizes of bulk carriers.

## Coal

Coal accounted for about 155 million tonnes of shipments in 1979. Over two thirds of coal shipped is for use in the world's steel industry, the remainder being steaming coal for use in energy related industries. These figures show a change over the last ten years in the pattern of coal shipments. The amount of steaming coal was falling in total tonnage terms until the oil crisis of 1972/73 but since then shipments have steadily increased. Coking shipments are closely controlled by the needs of the world's steel industry and there is very close co-operation between steel companies, mining companies and shipping interests. Close co-operation does, however, make coking coal trade very vulnerable to the state of the world economy which in turn has large effects on the steel industry.

All classes of coal are liable to spontaneous heating with the attendant risk of fire and explosion. The ship operator must take precautions against heat build up as with plenty of oxygen present, the coal will ignite. Heat is dispersed by ventilation but this in itself can be a hazard with coal as ventilation introduces more oxygen into the hold.

Freshly mined coal can emit a gas which, when mixed with oxygen, forms an explosive mixture and must be removed by surface ventilation. The final problem is damage to machinery caused by coal dust; precautions must be taken when loading and discharging to minimise its spread.

Ship loaders fed by conveyors are used extensively and in some places gantries tip full rail wagons into the vessel. Discharge is by high capacity grabs with loading rates of 8,000 tonnes per hour and discharge rates of up to 3,000 tonnes per hour. Coal handling ports have been up-graded in the last few years with better handling facilities and wider and deeper approach channels and berths to accommodate larger bulk carriers.

## Bauxite/Alumina

Bauxite is the raw material used in the aluminium industry. There is an increasing trend for bauxite to undergo intermediate refining close to the mining areas to change to alumina and reduce the amount of waste material carried on the ship. Bauxite is fairly dense with a stowage factor of 0.7m$^3$/tonne; alumina stows at 1.2m$^3$/tonne. Tonnages carried show a steady increase over the past decade due to the increasing use of aluminium by the manufacturing industry.

Sea carriage of bauxite/alumina is not problematic except for the correct distribution of the payload around the ship. During loading and discharging precautions must be taken to minimise the spread of dust.

Loading is generally by travelling conveyors and covered shutes to reduce dust. Discharge is by grab with loading rates able to reach 3,000 tonnes/hour and discharge rates of up to 1,500 tonnes/hour.

## Secondary Bulk Trades

There are many other commodities carried in bulk and these are usually categorised into two groups — minor bulk and neo-bulk.

Minor bulk includes cargoes such as manganese, nickel, crome, concentrates of copper, lead, zinc and fertilisers, many of which are shipped in relatively small parcels and provide employment for smaller size bulk carriers and conventional tween deck tramps.

Neo-bulk cargoes include iron and steel products, scrap vehicles and forest products. In many cases these cargoes are carried in specifically designed ships but they are all traditional liner cargoes and still play a significant role in liner shipping.

The foregoing brief description of some of the major commodities carried in the dry bulk market srves to illustrate that a major factor in the design of a bulk carrier is the type of commodity that the ship will transport. The stowage factor, commodity characteristics and handling method will limit the designer in the choice of materials and the general arrangement of the ship. The other main elements that must be considered are the trade route with the constraint of the port facilities at each end and the quantity of cargo flowing over that route. There is much evidence to suggest that, within these constraints, the shipowner will attempt to take advantage of economies of scale by using the largest ship possible on any given route.

## FURTHER READING

Cargo Systems Research, *Grain: Seaborne Trade, Transportation and Handling*, Cargo Systems Research Consultants Ltd, Surrey, England, 1978.

I.M.C.O., *Code of Safe Practice For Solid Bulk Cargoes*, No. 80.10.E, I.M.C.O., London, 1978.

Thomas, R.E., *Stowage: The Properties and Stowage of Cargo*, Brown Son & Ferguson, Glasgow, 1981.

# 6 Bulk Carriers

Since the 1950's there has been a change in the methods used by the shipping industry to carry dry bulk commodities. The changes have been caused by the increase in world economic activity — with its growth in productive capacity demanding greater quantities of raw materials — and partly to better methods of ship design and construction. World growth has led to a greater volume of world trade, the emergence of new sources of raw materials and a build up of new or less traditional manufacturing centres. The raw materials needed to sustain this upsurge in manufacturing were offered for shipment in much larger volumes than before and increasingly at regular almost scheduled intervals. The shipping industry sought technical and managerial solutions to meet the challenge of this growing volume of trade over long distances.

Traditionally, most bulk commodities were carried in ships known as tramps with tween-decks which were not only suitable for full ship bulk cargo charters but could be hired by liner shipping companies to help smooth peak demand. It became apparent to the shipping industry that there was an urgent need to design and build specifically designated ships for the efficient carriage of bulk commodities in large volumes. To a large extent this ended one of the traditional trading opportunities for bulk carrying ships — namely hiring into the liner trades at peak periods.

It is very difficult to make general comments about the bulk trades and the ships designed to carry the commodities concerned with them, as every cargo has different handling requirements and shipment flows. Some trade flows are concentrated on a few heavily used routes between a small number of highly developed ports which are closely controlled by the industrial companies that use the raw materials. Others are dispersed and (especially with agricultural products) are worldwide with the quantities and destination affected by climate and political crises. These two ends of the spectrum of services have resulted in very different situations at trade route terminals. When demand for a particular commodity is regular over a long period, investment has been undertaken in port facilities in order that larger and more efficient ships can be used: when demand is irregular there is no incentive to invest in port facilities, thus the ships must be more flexible and able to meet the demands of differing handling methods.

It is apparent that the type and size of ship used on a particular trade route to carry a particular commodity depends to a large extent on the conditions found in the ports served. One fact is indisputable, in that wherever possible, the largest ship able to use the ports and carry the cargo is used and all the large vessels are bulk carriers. Approximately 70% of all dry bulk cargo is carried in bulk carriers as opposed to the conventionally constructed tween deck ship: 95% of all iron ore, 80% of coal, 90% of grain, 70% of bauxite and 60% of phosphate rock. Some bulk carriers are called combined carriers as they are able to alternate between dry and liquid bulk cargoes. These will be discussed in a later chapter. In the past a significant amount of grain has been carried in tankers, but this seems to be declining.

## Bulk Carriers

The term bulk carrier has never been adequately defined but it is generally taken to be a single deck ship exceeding 122 metres in length with the engines aft. Many bulk carriers have special trimming devices for the cargo, are strengthened to take the stress induced by the cargo being shot into the holds by gravity and are designed for discharge by grabs.

## General Bulk Carrier

The general bulk carrier is designed to ship all types of bulk cargo as economically as possible within the limitations imposed by the characteristics of the commodity carried. The hold is structured, (see Figure 6.1) in order that the cargo is self trimming, by sloping the hold deck upwards and outwards to form a side wing tank in the bilge; the upper part of the hold slopes downwards and outwards from the deckhead to form an upper wing tank. The lower wing tanks are used for water ballast; the upper can be used for water ballast or

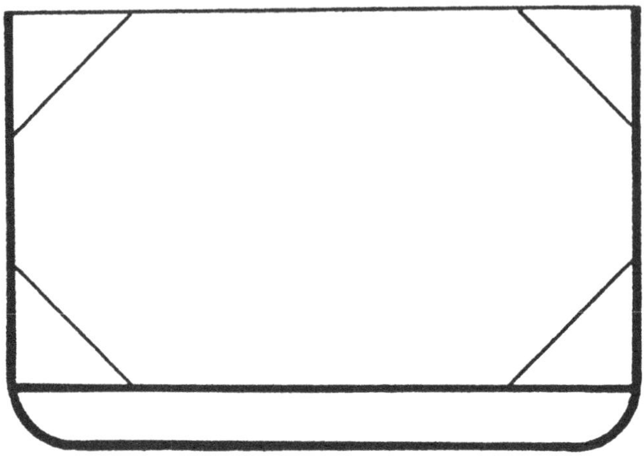

FIGURE 6.1. Cross section through general bulk carrier hold

cargo as required. A deep double bottom tank provides space for fuel, fresh water and ballast. The holds are entered via large hatch openings in the deck which are made water-tight by large steel covers. Invariably, the hatches are served by ships cargo handling gear in the form of derricks or cranes. These ships are designed to be very versatile as to the commodity they can carry and the ports to which they may have to operate.

The size of a general bulk carrier is not solely determined by the technical competence of the ship building industry but more by the specific requirements of the operational pattern they are expected to undertake. It must always be borne in mind by all people working within the industry that shipping is only a sub-system of the total transport network which is designed to service the industrial system of the world. There are restrictions on the size of vessel to be used in any situation governed by outside factors. When purely considering the shipping part of the total transport chain, canal widths, port approach channel widths and depths, berth capacities and berth lengths dictate the overall size of the ship that can trade in a particular area. Berth handling equipment and facilities will dictate the size of ship. The availability of land for storage and the capacity of inland transport modes will have an effect on the amount of cargo available for shipment at any one time. A number of examples will suffice to illustrate this point.

Within the limits imposed by the factors mentioned above, shipowners and cargo shippers will try to take advantage of any scale economies that may be possible. It is generally accepted that the Panama Canal has imposed severe limitations on the size of many general bulk carriers and has led to the design of 'Panamax' vessels. The maximum dead weight of a vessel using the canal is restricted to between 50,000 and 70,000 tonnes depending on beam and draft; the maximum beam is 106 feet. A lot of ingenuity has been shown by ship designers in trying to fit as much payload as possible within ships with external dimensions that are limited by the canal capacity.

The coal route from the U.S. East coast to the Far East is constrained by draft restrictions at the loading ports (although deep water terminals are being constructed) and the Panama Canal locks. Only 60,000 tonnes of coal per ship can be carried on this route so shipowners are investigating the route via Southern Africa. Much larger cargoes could be carried around Cape Horn: however, not only are there few deep water terminals available for large ships, but the voyage length is over 5,000 miles longer. Only when the cost per tonne carried is comparable between the two routes is there any incentive to use the longer route. These limitations mean that there is a grouping of general bulk carriers around a certain deadweight level.

Another grouping of ships with a lifting capacity of between 25,000 and 30,000 tonne deadweight is known as *handy sized bulk carriers*. The purpose of these ships is to achieve maximum trading opportunities for their owners within the limitations imposed by the majority of world ports. The size limitations make the need for very flexible ships paramount: ships that can carry almost any bulk commodity to almost any port in the world. The operating system for these small bulk carriers requires the traditional tramp shipping management to take advantage of trading opportunities wherever in the world ships happen to be when cargo is on offer.

Cargo shippers and shipowners are united in striving to benefit from economies of scale, but their efforts are limited by factors beyond the control of the shipping industry. Many factors are historical — port sites and industrial complexes were developed before the technology was available to dramatically increase the size of ships. Increasing the depth of approach channels and berthing areas is very costly and in many cases, physically impossible. Hence the continuing need for small ships to service certain ports. In addition, some commodities are not produced in quantities large enough to warrant large ships, again giving opportunities for smaller bulk carrier types.

The pattern of grain trading can be used to illustrate factors that are beyond even elementary planning. The ports used for grain trading vary from the very sophisticated using pneumatic and conveyor systems to large storage silos, to the very basic ports using ships gear and grabs straight into lorries or barges. Port types reflect the regularity of shipments to them which in turn dictate the level of investment in equipment, for example with irregular grain shipments the port facilities can be very basic indeed.

Thus the type of port facilities available depends on the regularity of shipments. All these factors dictate the type and size of bulk carrier used on any one trade route.

## Specialised Bulk Carriers

It is impossible to describe in detail all the various types of specialised bulk carrier within the pages of a book of this type. The design of specialised bulk carriers, although linked to the basic principles underlying development of all bulk carriers, is concerned with overcoming problems associated with handling, carriage and care of a particular commodity. The design process begins, not from providing as many trading opportunities for the owner as possible, but from the shipping requirements of the cargo carried.

The heavy ore carrier has no problems in loading to its design draft as only a small proportion of the potential cargo carrying volume will be needed to accommodate the cargo. The technical problem to overcome is in distributing the payload around the ship in order that reasonable stability is maintained. The structure is designed to withstand the force generated by this distribution. Heavy ore ships are designed with specially strengthened ore holds built over a very deep double bottom which raise the centre of gravity of the cargo (Figure 6.2). There are wing tanks running the full length and depth of the ship which can be used for water ballast.

The majority of large ore carriers are owned or directly operated for the benefit of large industrial and mining companies. They are in

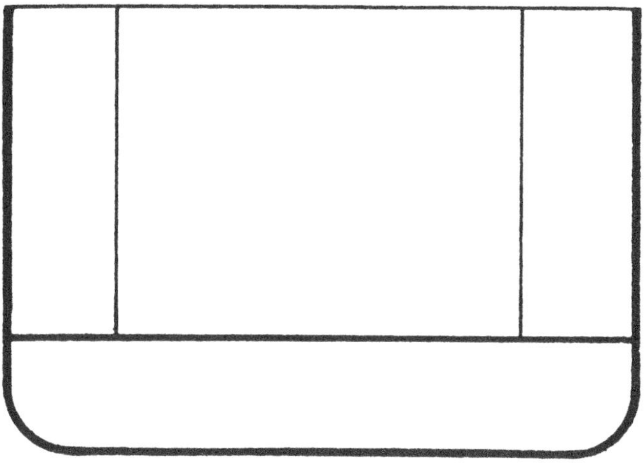

FIGURE 6.2. Cross section through specialized iron ore carrier hold

the main used on a few regular routes, transporting basic ore from the mining area to the steel making plants. Their design and trading pattern mean that they spend a large proportion of their time in ballast.

In contrast, there is no possibility of a conventional bulk carrier loading wood chips and being down to design draft with a full deadweight cargo. Wood chip carriers are designed with large freeboard to draft ratios in order to accommodate a reasonable cargo. Again, the design is a function of the commodity carried.

## Tramp Ships

The term tramp ship is used in this context to describe vessels which are conventional in the sense that they are tween-deck ships and in appearance are similar to the liner ships described in Chapter 2. They are built without any specific cargo or trade in mind and can carry any bulk commodity or mixture of commodities on offer in any port in the world. They have the ability to contract into the liner trades at times of peak liner demand and so relieve liner owners of some of the burden of fluctuations in shipping demand. Much of the bulk commodity trade discussed in Chapter 5 has now been accommodated in bulk carriers but there remains a large fleet of traditional tramp ships which offer their services through the shipping exchanges.

The similarity of the traditional tramp to the cargo liner is striking. There are a number of holds thoughout its length, split by a tween deck into upper and lower sections with a double bottom tank running the full length under the main holds. The holds are rather larger in size than those on a similar cargo liner and in most cases there is no deep tank. The cargo handling gear is much simpler, consisting of derricks at each hatch. The fuller form of tramp allows a greater deadweight lifting capability than the cargo liner and its slower speed leads to lower running costs.

## The Ships

The tramp shipping sector of the industry was dominated in the 1950's by one type of ship known as the "Liberty". These vessels were built during the second world war using the new technique of welding and the mass production system of assembling pre-fabricated units at the building berth. The "Liberty" was the first so called "standard" ship and had a speed of 10 to 11 knots and could lift approximately 10,000 tonnes of cargo.

The "Liberty" was not intended for long service but to fill the gaps left by shipping losses during the war hence the standard design and the mass production techniques. From the late 1950's the rising cost of maintenance and insurance caused shipping companies to withdraw many from service. The "Liberty" had proved a huge success during its lifetime and had proved the worth of standard designs for ships in the bulk cargo trades. This success and the diminishing numbers still trading led shipping companies and ship builders to research the economics of building standard, mass produced vessels to replace the "Liberty".

The subsequent research suggested the need for a flexible, multipurpose vessel, no larger than 15,000 deadweight, which should carry full or part bulk cargoes to most world ports and charter into the liner trades if and when required.

The ships that followed were called standard designs by the ship builders (although many people in the industry think of them as

"Liberty ship replacements"). There are a number of benefits — claimed by advocates of standard designs — which have been used as the basis for their research, development and construction.

- The original ship cost is lower as series production allows development costs to be spread over a long production run and scheduling can be carefully managed and planned.
- There is the possibility of early ship delivery because the design is pre-developed and production line methods — using pre-fabricated standard parts reduce the time taken to build the ship once an order has been placed.
- A standard design is said to lead to a ship that matches its intended market. This means that the shipping company should have no difficulty in finding employment for the vessel once its merits are established.
- There are cost savings to be gained from outfitting and spares as the cost of procuring the necessary items is spread across a large fleet of ships.
- The performance of the ship is enhanced by the concentration of design and development effort into a single type of vessel which is fitted to the needs of industry as a whole rather than one shipping company's needs. (On the other hand, this could be taken as a disadvantage by ship owners in that too great a compromise must be made to fit a ship to the needs of general industry rather than their individual requirements).
- There can be significant gains in operation efficiency and safety if standard designs are grouped in fleets so that operating personnel become familiar with the ships (this is a very valid point as many nations' sailors spend short periods at sea and frequently change ship). It does, however, mean that the ship owner must adhere to the standard arrangement and not change the specification either by adding too much extra equipment or by making excessive modifications.

As can be seen from Figure 6.3, standard ships are conventional in that they are designed with two decks, a double bottom, and derricks as standard cargo handling gear. With all types there is a range of 'extras' that can be added at the owner's request.

The two most successful standard ships are the "S.D.14" and the "Freedom" built by Austin and Pickersgiel and I.H.I. respectively.

Table 6.1 gives a comparison between the Liberty, S.D. 14 and Freedom class ships.

Most standard design builders offer each shipowner the chance to change the specification and add more sophisticated equipment. This is recognition that the type of equipment required for individual ships and different companies must be a product of the trade flows and port facilities likely to be encountered on any given route.

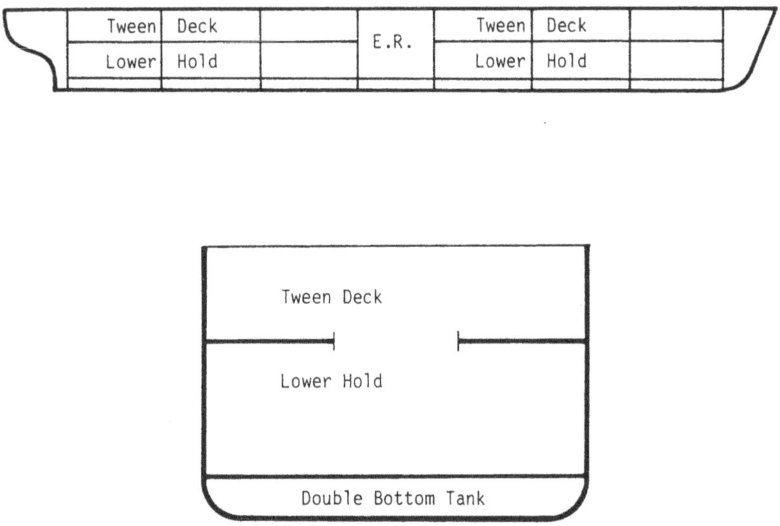


FIGURE 6.3. General arrangement of holds in standard design tramp ship

TABLE 6.1
COMPARISON OF THE MAIN PARAMETERS OF LIBERTY, S.D. 14 AND FREEDOM

| Type | Liberty | S.D. 14 | Freedom |
|---|---|---|---|
| Length | 143 m | 141 m | 143 m |
| Draft | 9.05 m | 8.84 m | 9.05 m |
| Grain Capacity | | 21641 $m^3$ | |
| Deadweight | 10000 Tonnes | 14910 Tonnes | 14800 Tonnes |
| Speed | 11 knots | 14.9 knots | 13.5 knots |

With the takeover of much bulk trading by bulk carriers, it must seem strange to many readers that the conventional tramp, as represented by the standard ship, has any role left in the shipping industry. There seems plenty of scope, however, for the multi-purpose conventional cargo ship in the minor bulk sector and in conventional break bulk operations where unitised cargo systems have not been instituted.

## Charter Shipping

Dry bulk shipping services are bought and sold in the main commercial centres of the world at shipping exchanges. One of the major shipping markets is the Baltic Exchange in London and this operates to very simple principles. Ship brokers acting on behalf of shipowners on the one hand and cargo shippers on the other, meet at the Exchange daily at pre-arranged times to negotiate the carriage of bulk commodities by the world's dry bulk fleet. The shipowner's broker is looking for a cargo to fill his ship at a freight rate that will enable the shipowner to at least cover costs, while the cargo shipper's broker is looking for a ship of the right type and size to carry the tonnage of a commodity between named ports, at a set time, so that he can carry out his contractual obligations as cheaply as possible. In many ways the bulk shipping exchanges are the closest any trading system comes to operating under conditions of *perfect competition* as there are a large number of small sized buyers and a large number of small sized sellers. At most times there is no one organisation that can dominate the market and so influence the prices charged unduly. There are also very few barriers to entry to the market and any new entrants can produce identical services to established firms. Any technical innovation must prove its worth to the shipowner by enabling him to secure a better deal in the market and to the shipper in providing the service that he requires. There is no point in building highly advanced ships if either the shippers do not require sophistication or are unwilling to pay higher prices.

The freight rate levels are governed in the main by the level of supply and demand at any given time. If there are more ships available than cargoes to be carried, rates tend to be low: if there are more cargoes than ships, rates tend to be high. Management skill in the bulk shipping charter sector is expressed by the ability to anticipate demand for shipping services worldwide — charters are arranged between places with a high shipping demand to avoid long ballast passages. Management skill is also reflected in the ability to anticipate requirements of ship sizes and have appropriate ships available at the right times. Some shipowners make their living by anticipating the needs of the market and buying or selling ships as the price of tonnage fluctuates.

## Types of Charter

There are a number of different charter arrangements that can be negotiated between shippers and shipowners. The ship can be chartered *bareboat*, that is with the crew and management supplied by the charterer or as a combination where the charterer and shipowner agree as to who supplies what.

The simplest charter is the "voyage charter" in that the ship is chartered for one voyage to carry a particular parcel of cargo between two named ports. A variation of this is where the ship is chartered for a number of consecutive voyages. The freight rate at so much per tonne of cargo is agreed between the shipowner and the cargo shipper and takes account of the prevailing market rate and the availability of other ships. Other clauses in the contract concern the state of the ship with regard to structure, the commodity to be carried, time allowed for carriage and handling, disputes settling provisions and the legal regime under which the bargain is struck. The resulting freight rates are published by leading shipping analysts and time series are produced to give an indication of market trends.

Time charters are the method by which a cargo shipper secures the services of a particular ship for a term usually of between 1-5 years. The time charter gives the shipowner security of employment over a lengthy period but the rate will be fixed at the start of the term and will prevent the shipowner making good profits in boom times. The clauses in the charter are agreed between the parties.

Contracts of Affreightment are contracts signed by the shipowner with a commodity importing company to deliver specified amounts of that commodity between named ports at specified intervals. The vessel to be used is not specified so the shipping company can schedule its ships to get optimum use of its fleet by combining several of these charters and voyage charters. Contracts of affreightment type charters led to the formation of bulk shipping pools or consortia (as in container shipping, mentioned in Chapter 3).

Bulk shipping covers a wide sphere of ship types from small conventional ships designed to carry any commodity to any port, to the large specialised ore carriers designed to carry iron ore efficiently, in very large quantities, between a few highly developed ports. The management skills, operating techniques and technical sophistication depend to an extent on the type of commodity carried and the regularity of shipments.

## FURTHER READING

Dewry, H.P., *Future of the Large Bulk Carrier Shipping*, Shipping Study No. 91, 1981. *Changing Ships Type/Size Preference in the Dry Bulk Market*, Shipping Study No. 81, 1981. The Trading Prospects for 'Panamax' Bulk Carriers and O.B.O's., Shipping Study No. 83, 1981. *Deep Sea Trade and the Transportation of the Forest Products*, Shipping Study No. 73, 1980. H.P. Dewry Shipping Publications, London.

Mextas, B.N., *The Economics of Tramp Shipping*, Athlone Press, London, 1971.

U.S. Government, *Development of a standard U.S. Flag Dry Bulk Carrier*, P.B. 293 369, U.S. Government, Washington.

Williamson, G.A., The Principle Dimensions and Operating Drafts of Bulk Carriers, Marine Transport Centre, University of Liverpool, Liverpool, 1978.

# 7 The Tanker Trades

## Historical Review

The first reported commercial oil well was drilled in Pennsylvania in 1859 and was the forerunner of a vast industry that has subsequently grown to dominate the world's political, economic and industrial relationships. The product sought from that first oil well was Kerosene used in domestic lighting, heating and cooking while the rest of the crude oil was either burnt on site or thrown away. As with all raw materials, research was undertaken into possible uses for the by-products of Kerosene production which later resulted in the petrochemical industry.

The first wells were fairly shallow and easy to drill. However, the need of the world's economy for energy generating raw materials has led to large scale exploration and wells are now drilled to depths of up to twenty thousand feet. The search for new sources of oil has spread from land based sites to ocean depths. One highly specialised section of the shipping industry is the operation and design of oil rig supply vessels which serve exploration rigs. A study of this shipping sector is part of the oil exploration field and is therefore, outside the scope of this book.

The major areas for oil production change as discovery of new oil fields result from constant exploration. Russia and the United States dominated the early decades of the oil industry (although oil was discovered in Mexico and the Middle East in the 1920's). The discoveries of vast reserves in the Arab countries in the 1950's has now made the Middle Eastern countries the major suppliers of the world's oil needs. As exploration and production technology developed, it became possible to explore the sea bed and led to a growing number of offshore sites. All oil-related discoveries change the pattern of oil movements and the types of ships needed.

The first ships carrying oil were sailing vessels with cargoes of oil in casks. This type of cargo was considered highly dangerous as leakage from the barrels caused gas pockets to form in the holds and other enclosed spaces. When there was a build up of gas all naked lights had to be extinguished to avoid the risk of explosion. There is some dispute among maritime historians regarding the first vessel specifically designed to carry oil in bulk, using the ship's hull as the container and steam pumps to discharge the cargo. It is generally taken that the "Gluckauf" launched in 1886 was the first oil tanker, a sail assisted steamer with the engines aft and a cofferdam between the engine room and the oil cargo.

## Trading Patterns

Trading patterns or route systems used by the world's tanker fleet are a direct consequence of world energy demand, the source of production or oil field sites and the location of crude oil processing plant or refineries. In addition, the development of ship building technology dictates the type of commodity that can be carried, the size of individual consignments, the handling method and the range of commodities carried on the same voyage in one ship. As will be seen in the following chapters, these factors combine to govern the nature of the tanker fleet at any given moment.

Global energy demand is dictated by economic activity. At times of growth in the world's economy, oil demand rises; in times of recession, oil demand falls. Times of slump and boom cause planning difficulties in the sea transport sector. It must be remembered that oil is not just the basis for energy industries, but is feed stock for chemical and plastic industries. The trading pattern of tankers is affected by the need to connect sources of production with areas of consumption. Historically, major consumers of oil such as N.W. Europe who have little oil within their own region, have had to import all their needs from producing areas. As new sources of oil are discovered and developed, new manufacturing sites are built and traditional trading patterns change.

Crude oil as produced at the well head is a raw material which must be processed. Processing (known as refining) produces energy related products such as gasoline and feed stock for chemical processes. Refineries were traditionally sited close to the oil wells and oil products were shipped to the consuming countries in product tankers.

As oil refining techniques developed and further research led to a demand for different products, more tankers were needed. Shipping technology at this time favoured the building of relatively small ships (in today's terms) with associated high transportation costs. High costs lead to high freight rates which must be absorbed by high value cargoes.

In the late 1940's there was a significant change in the planning of the location of the world's refining capacity. Much coal fired generating equipment, industrial plant and domestic heating appliances were replaced by oil related plant and the type of materials demanded by manufacturing processes (developed from crude oil refining) caused a growth in refinery located industrial plant.

The net result — a shift to the refining of crude oil from the production to the consuming areas — can be accounted for under four main headings.

- increased demand for oil in industrial countries
- political instability in producing countries
- growth of the petro-chemical industries
- economies of scale.

## Increased Demand for Energy

Increasing consumerism has led to an acceleration in demand for energy. Energy use increased by 1.5% in the 1920's and 1930's, by 5% in the 1950's, 5.5% in the 1960's and was increasing by 7% until the world recession started to affect the picture in 1979. Coal production during most of this time stayed virtually static; this shows that the major proportion of the world's energy needs were met by oil. There are large differences in energy consumption per head of population between countries, the U.S.A. being by far the leading user (and recently becoming a net importer of crude oil).

## Political Instability

A parallel development to the world's increasing reliance on oil to produce energy, has been the shift of oil production sources from the

U.S.A./Caribbean area to the Middle East and other countries. These new sources tend to be in countries that have a reputation for being politically unstable. The greater use of oil in relation to industry, led large users of oil to begin to locate refining capacity in the more controllable environment of the consuming countries. Besides control, the policy gave oil companies flexibility in choosing their oil source and mixing crude oil from different sources provided a sound base for product production and for amassing strategic reserves. The siting of oil refineries is once again in the balance as producing countries gain political influence and economic strength based on revenues from the oil they ship. There is a strong incentive for these countries to build up an industrial base to take the place of oil when the oil recourse base runs dry. A first step is to attempt to locate refineries closer to the source of oil and distribute oil-related products.

### Growth of Petro-Chemical Industries

There has been a very strong trend over the last thirty years to replace much of the raw material used in manufacturing by oil-related or oil based products. In countries with a large manufacturing base this has led to the growth of the petro-chemical industries. The refining and petro-chemical processes are closely related so it is essential that they are located together. In addition it makes economic and trading sense to have chemical plants close to the markets that they serve.

### Economies of Scale

There is a relationship between technological progress in oil processing and refining capacity location on a world scale. As technology has advanced and more products are produced from a given quantity of oil, the need for larger refineries to economically handle the requirements of industrial demand has arisen. This requirement is furthered by the need to mix oil from different oil fields to produce the correct refining blend. Large refineries demand high levels of throughput of crude oil in order to achieve economies of scale and lower production costs. Whatever the reasons for location, strategic, economic or industrial, a constant flow of crude oil is required to feed the process. This demands either a large fleet of small tankers or a smaller fleet of very large tankers. Economies of scale can be achieved in oil carriage by carrying crude oil in vast tankers — the costs of carriage per tonne of cargo fall as the size of the tanker increases. This fall results from the capital cost of a tanker rising at a slower rate than the added tonnage: crew and maintenance costs are easily absorbed by carrying larger cargoes. The technology to build large vessels to carry crude oil developed quickly and changed the whole pattern of oil movements.

It is a much simpler management task to schedule regular supplies of crude oil in large individual quantities to a few large market based refineries than to try and schedule much smaller individual quantities of products from larger refineries (located close to oil production sites) to many small customers. These small parcels of products can be distributed over short distances from regional refineries by smaller ships. Cargoes of crude oil in transit can be easily diverted from one destination to another in order to overcome refining capacity problems and smooth out seasonal fluctuations in demand.

All the above factors have led to oil transportation by the large crude carriers that now predominate in tanker fleets. Only approximately 20% of the world tanker tonnage is engaged in the distribution of products; the remaining ships in crude. The change from carriage of refined products to carriage of crude has resulted in the building of larger tankers; but the major route for the oil trade from the Arabian Gulf to N.W. Europe was through the Red Sea, Suez Canal and Mediterranean. As in the case of certain bulk carriers, the Suez Canal imposed size limitations as can be seen by the fact that in 1960 the largest ships on this route were of approximately 65,000 dead weight tonnes.

Two significant events occurred to alter trade route patterns and ship size calculations allied to advances in shipbuilding and materials technology which has led to the design of some of the largest self propelled structures the world has ever seen.

- The Japanese economy expanded very rapidly in the 1950's leading to the demand for vast quantities of imported raw materials, especially iron ore for their steel industry and crude oil for energy generation. Unlike the route from the Arabian Gulf to N.W. Europe where size was restricted by limits imposed by the Suez Canal, there were no real physical barriers to ship size to serve the route to Japan.

Japanese shipyards set out to build not only large tankers but much simpler designs for the exclusive carriage of crude oil. In 1959 the "Universe Apollo" came into service between the Arabian Gulf and Japan capable of carrying 100,000 tonnes of oil. By 1965 the largest ship serving Japanese ports was the "Indemitusic Maru" able to carry over 200,000 tonnes of oil.

• The Japanese example demonstrated the economies of scale made possible by using large tankers to carry crude oil. The major oil companies undertook studies into the economies of carrying crude oil to N.W. Europe via the Southern Africa route with a view to freeing the European market from the size limits set by the Suez Canal. The studies resulted in the ordering of tankers able to carry 200,000 tonnes of oil for the N.W. Europe market: when the Suez Canal was closed in the late 1960's this pattern of operation had to be adopted by all tanker owners.

## Ownership Patterns

The oil industry is very integrated, the major oil companies controlling the whole process including the shipping part of the business. The result: the majority of shipping movements involving tankers are closely supervised by oil companies either owning the tankers directly or chartering them on long or short term contracts. There are fluctuations in the demand for oil shipment so the transport departments of the major oil companies must strike a balance between the amount of wholly owned and chartered tonnage. The large own account sector does mean that the oil companies have a large influence over the design of tankers.

There is a definite split between the carriage of crude oil and the carriage of oil-related products. Chapters 8, 9 and 10 will be used to discuss these parts of the system.

# 8 Crude Carriers

An oil tanker is specifically designed to carry liquid cargoes in bulk, with the main engines aft away from the cargo carrying portion of the ship's hull for greater safety. It has only one deck, no double bottom tank beneath the main portion of the ship and a carrying area divided into oil tight compartments: the hull, ship's bottom, deck and tank bulkheads are used as the containment barrier. The deck is penetrated by small apertures for taking cargo measurements. Loading and discharge is via a pipeline system which runs along the tank bottom with oil flow controlled by valves which can be used to fill the appropriate tanks in a certain order.

The sections that follow discuss the technological and operational solutions to the problems posed by very large crude carriers.

## Loading

The ship's pipeline system is connected to the shore system at the ship's pipeline manifold by flexible steel hoses or a loading arm. The shore personnel control the delivery of the oil and will obey all instructions from the ship's personnel as to speed of delivery and stopping the flow. The pipeline system on board the ship is arranged to allow oil into the tanks by opening the required valves. At first, loading is at a relatively slow rate in order that all connections, pipelines and cargo compartments can be checked for leaks and ensure that loading is proceeding properly. Once the checks have been carried out, the full loading rate can be used.

The loading sequence of cargo compartments must be well planned.

- A logical sequence of tanks is followed to enable the personnel involved to control the operation easily. Only one or two tanks reach the maximum load level at a time and there is always one empty tank close to the tank being filled so that when the loading tank is reaching its maximum level, oil can be transferred slowly to it.

- To plan the sequence of tanks to be loaded so that there are no excessive stresses on the ship's structure (built up if all the cargo is loaded at one end of the ship with the tanks at the other empty) all tankers carry instruction booklets and many have balance machines which calculate the stresses automatically.

When loading is finished, the cargo in each tank is measured and total cargo on board calculated. All tanks are checked for water content, specific gravity of the oil and samples taken for analysis. The surplus oil in the connecting hoses is blown into the ship's tanks by compressed air and all valves closed. Pipes lead from the top of each tank to pressure regulated valves which allow any excess gas generated during the voyage to escape into the atmosphere.

## Discharge

Discharge of crude oil presents very few problems for the vessel's crew unless involved in handling a volatile cargo. The ship arrives at the discharging berth and is connected to the shore by flexible hoses. The internal pipeline system is made ready by opening the appropriate valves and ships pumps are used to transfer the cargo to the shore. The order of discharge is planned, with due regard to any likely stresses to the ship's structure and the need to maintain a head of oil in the after part of the tank above the pump suction. Speed of discharge is limited by a combination of the speed of the ship's pumps and the pressure generated by pushing the oil along the shore pipelines. The last drop of crude from each tank has to be stripped ashore by special pumps that will operate when air is mixed with the oil.

After discharge, the ship must load sea water ballast to sink the ship sufficiently to undertake the voyage back to the loading port safely and economically. This poses problems for tankers which have to load ballast into tanks which have carried crude oil as the ballast must be clean if it is to be discharged into the sea in port. The problems of disposing of dirty ballast will be discussed later.

## Large Crude Carriers

What constitutes a large carrying tanker is a matter for debate and, obviously, changes with the passage of time. The two definitions generally accepted in the oil industry as classifying these ships are; (1) a very large crude carrier, (VLCC) is defined as an oil tanker able to carry more than 160,000 tonnes of cargo and (2) an ultra large crude carrier, (ULCC) defined as an oil tanker able to carry more than 400,000 tonnes of cargo. These large tankers are (with a few mobile oil rigs) the largest self-propelled structures ever built by man and there is no doubt that they are the most economical method of moving large quantities of raw materials over very long distances. Indeed, there is a lot of evidence to suggest that in terms of tonne miles, the VLCC has the lowest accident rate of any freight carrying vehicle.

The development of these large ships has, however, brought many problems. These are reflected in world opinion outside of the shipping industry and have led to pressure for change in management and environmental practices. The problems and their solutions can, for the sake of clarity of discussion, be split into four closely related areas: operating restrictions, explosion hazards, pollution hazards and corrosion. A study of these areas will illustrate the way in which technological advance has been used and the changing nature of operational practices has been utilised to smooth the voyages for the benefit of populations energy needs.

## Operating Restrictions

To increase the cargo carrying capacity of a ship, the outside dimensions must be increased to expand the internal cubic. It is not necessary to increase all dimensions in exact proportion, for example, length and breadth can be enlarged while leaving draft constant. However, there are penalties to be paid in respect of the propulsive power needed from the engine per tonne of cargo carried (and service speed from the changed underwater shape of the ship) which means that all dimensions must be increased to some extent. There comes a point when the draft becomes too much for certain well used trade routes with shallow water.

Certain narrow strips of water (like the Dover Straits) which lie between loading and discharge ports cause navigational problems for large ships with regard to their manoeuvrability in heavy traffic areas and the changing nature of the sea bed. A large ship takes much longer to stop, needs more room to turn than its smaller counterpart and, because of draft restrictions, often has to keep to a limited track owing to sea bed conditions. The need to avoid manoeuvring calls for knowledge of the depth of water available to the ship at any time, accurate information on tidal ranges and current systems, precise data on the changes in the sea bed topography over time and sufficient navigational aids to fix its position. The increased need for accurate information has resulted in a growth in the study of oceanography and the development of marine survey techniques.

It must be noted that many oil refinery sites were developed on the banks of river estuaries close to other industrial complexes — alongside what have now become relatively shallow waterways. Indeed, many refineries are completely inaccessible to today's large oil carriers. The accumulated investment in plant and labour expertise make it impossible to re-locate these industrial complexes closer to deeper water and there is a limit in both physical and financial terms to the amount of dredging that can be undertaken to deepen the approach channels to these berths. These difficulties must be overcome by developing shipping systems that can take advantage of the economies of scale inherent in operating large tankers. At the same time the crude oil must be delivered in such a way that large ships can be used for the long trunk haul and relatively smaller ships used for distribution to the refinery. There are three methods used to operate a trunking/local delivery: transhipment, lightering and deep water sea berths.

## Transhipment

Transhipment involves the use of an intermediate port where deep draft ships can discharge the oil into storage tanks. The oil is then loaded onto shallower draft tankers for distribution to oil refineries. There are economic penalties in not using the deep draft tanker for the whole voyage. However, the penalty is small when compared to the cost of re-locating an oil refinery to accomodate the deeper draft ships. In some cases, it can introduce an element of flexibility to crude distribution between refineries in a region by planning the ship service from the transhipment port.

### Lightering and Lightening

Lightering and lightening operations have been used by the oil industry for a number of years to overcome draft limitations at both loading and discharge ports. The process is an extension of the method used by the world navies to supply ships at sea — the main difference is in the size of ships involved and the quantity of cargo that is transferred. Lightering and lightening operations are carried out in a sheltered bay, the mooring of the two ships being achieved with the ships underway after which the larger ship anchors. The ships are connected by flexible hose and it is standard practice for the lightering ships to control the transfer of oil. Lightering operations are very dependent on weather conditions and strict rules are laid down as to the sea state, wind and weather conditions that can be tolerated during the operation. Care is essential to avoid an oil spill with consequent pollution close to the coast; all ships involved in oil transfers at sea carry chemical dispersants and boats to spread them in the event of a spillage.

The distinction between lightering and lightening is that in the former the oil is transferred to smaller ships and the large tanker does not put into port: in the latter, sufficient oil is transferred to reduce the draft of the large tanker to allow the ship into a port with a draft limit.

### Sea Berths

Sea berths (similarly to lightering) have been used in many parts of the world where it is either economically or physically impossible to build a jetty. These systems require the ship to be moored in position by its own anchors forward with a carefully laid out pattern of mooring buoys at the stern. The ship picks up the pipeline from the sea bed for connection to the ship's manifold and the oil is discharged or loaded along a seabed pipeline. Communication is maintained between ship and shore by radio or telephone.

Large tankers that need deep water can use this type of berth, but there are problems. To overcome these, single point mooring structures have been developed where the ship moors by the bow which leaves it free to rotate whilst keeping its head to the prevailing wind and waves. The oil is transferred through a connecting hose either over the bow or floated to midships, through the centre of the structure and by underwater pipeline system to the refinery.

## Fire and Explosion Hazards

After discharging the oil cargo, the tanker must be prepared for its return to the loading port. This entails loading the vessel with ballast to a depth at which the propellor operates efficiently in order that it will not be damaged by bad weather and will retain its manoeuvring characteristics.

On arrival at the loading port, the ballast must be discharged — if discharged into the sea, the ballast water must be clean. This means that if oil carrying tanks are used for ballast, at some time during the voyage, the tank must be cleaned and clean ballast loaded. At the end of the discharge, the oil residue gives off a gas that fills the tanks. During the cleaning operation, this must be dispersed into the atmosphere to render the tanks gas free. The operation, must be carefully carried out as the gas/air mixture is volatile: it is during this time that a spark or naked light in or near the tanks is liable to cause an explosion and fire. A number of explosions and fires have occurred on tankers during the tank cleaning operation.

There are basically two solutions to the problem of explosive mixtures in an oil tanker's cargo compartments. One is to maintain a non-explosive mixture in the tanks at all times, the other is to make sure that there is no possibility of sparks or naked lights getting close to the explosive mixture.

The first solution is accomplished by replacing the gas/air mixture in the holds with some kind of inert gas which is supplied by using exhaust gas from the ship's boilers after having passed through a scrubbing and cleansing plant to remove solids and other impurities. Inert gas systems must be used in accordance with the manufacturers instructions as badly maintained and operated systems have caused corrosion to the piping system and the ship's tanks.

The second solution is more difficult as it is subject to human error and therefore vital that all ships personnel are thoroughly trained in tank cleaning procedures and the use of safe equipment. For example, the use of high pressure water jets through tank cleaning machine nozzles involves the risk of a build up of static electricity with the subsequent danger of a spark between the nozzle tip and the tank structure. To avoid the sparks, the machines must be earthed to the ship and the earthing bond checked at frequent intervals to make sure it is operational. Only by proper training can ships' crews be made aware of the dangers involved and the correct procedures to follow.

## Pollution

According to public opinion, pollution of the sea by crude oil is one of the major problems confronting mankind. This is not surprising given the very strong emotions generated at the sight of once beautiful sea birds being washed ashore covered in black oil or the sight of a stretch of golden sand covered in thick black oil. The depth of feeling is understandable in local communities where the whole economic base can be ruined overnight by oil pollution or the delicate balance of the ecological system of the oceans changed. It is no solution for the shipping industry to wash its hands of the problem and say that this is the price that the world must pay for its demand that oil be supplied. Fortunately, the shipping industry is constantly developing new methods to combat pollution hazards.

In short, there are two quite unrelated factors that together form the threat of pollution. The solution to the problem lies in consolidating the world's need for oil without the danger of polluting the world's oceans. The two factors are, firstly the deliberate discharge of oil (or in most cases, oil and water mixtures) into the sea during the tank cleaning operation and secondly, the release of oil into the ocean as a result of an accident which ruptures the ship's hull. The accident can result from either the ship running aground or a collision.

In the past the tank cleaning operation was accomplished by washing the tank with high pressure water jets and pumping the oil/water mixture over the side into the sea leaving a characteristic oil slick in the ship's wake. As the number and size of tankers increased, it was realized that this method was causing severe pollution to coasts close to well used tanker routes. Early attempts to contain the problem involved splitting up of the oceans into zones where oil could be discharged (or not) according to the ship's position. By this method it was hoped that the oil would be dispersed by the time it neared the shore. Since then, new techniques have been developed to combat the problem at source, namely aboard the ships themselves.

## Load on Top

During the ballast passage, the cargo tanks are cleaned using high pressure water jets in the normal fashion but the oil/water is left to separate, the oil floating on top of clean water. Clean sea water can than be pumped into the sea and the oil and the interface mixture left in the tank. Care must be taken to ensure that sufficient time has been allowed for the oil/water separation to take place and that only clean water is pumped into the ocean. The residual oil is pumped back into the tanks and mixed with the next cargo, which, on a crude carrier, causes very few problems of contamination. The ballast on board when the ship arrives in the loading port is clean and can therefore, be discharged.

## Crude Oil Washing

For some time, it has been apparent that sea water is not the best medium for washing the crude oil residues from tanks as the water leaves an oily film over the ship's structure which can contaminate clear ballast. Several chemical solvents have been tried in an effort to improve the cleaning process but, although they gave excellent results, they were expensive to use and added hazards to those already present. The crude oil washing system was developed to overcome these problems while improving the cleaning process at the same time. The tanks are washed during the discharge of the cargo by circulating crude oil through fixed spray nozzles, dislodging the remaining residue and resulting in very clean tanks.

If crude oil washing techniques are combined with an inert gas system and separate water ballast tanks, there is very little possibility of oil escape during cleaning or ballasting operations, or for an explosion to occur.

**I.M.O. and Pollution**

The clean ballast issue has been extensively debated throughout the shipping world, both by national assemblies and within the I.M.O. consultation machinery. The agreements reached will form an annexe or protocols to the 1973 Marine Pollution Convention and the 1974 Safety of Life at Sea Convention.

These requirements can be summarised as follows.

- New ships of over 20,000 dwt built to carry crude oil must be fitted with segregated ballast tanks, crude oil washing systems and inert gas systems. Segregated ballast means the provision of a system of tanks, pumps and pipelines which are completely separated from the cargo handling system and used permanently to carry and handle clean ballast water.
- The space available for ballast must be such that the ship can be operated in the ballast condition with safety. This means that there will be some less cargo carrying space resulting in a reduction in revenue potential for a given size of ship.

Complete adherence to these rules by the world's tanker fleet would virtually overcome the problem of pollution from tank cleaning operations.

The main problem is how to implement the spirit of these proposals when applying the rules to existing ships. The question is very complex and involves long negotiations in order to agree a set of rules that can be applied without then being too heavy a burden on the shipowner. At first, it was felt by many nations that after an adjustment period, (regulations had come into force) all ships should be fitted with segregated ballast tank systems. However, it was felt that this would impose grave financial burdens on many tanker owners. To alleviate this, it was decided to phase the proposals over a longer time span, leaving the shipowner the choice of whether to adopt a segregated or a separate system. A segregated system needs to be designed and built into the ship's existing space. Separate or nominated clean ballast tanks involve the nomination and the exclusive use of certain tanks for carrying clean ballast and the use of the ship's cargo lines and pumps, once they have been flushed, for loading and discharging the ballast. The nominated ballast tank system allows the shipowner to plan the ballast carrying system in line with maximum possible payload.

## Accidents

As mentioned previously, the second cause of pollution of the sea is due to oil spills resulting from ruptured plating. It is felt by many writers that these accidents can only be prevented by abandoning the traditional independent line taken by the industry and allowing direct government control over certain aspects of operations. The problem arises from control of very large tankers in coastal waters and in heavily trafficked sea lanes. Only governments working together in international organisations can adopt navigation rules that give large tankers added protection, sanction and monitor one way routing systems to cut down the need for large tankers to manoeuvre in confined and shallow water, and lay down regulations to keep large tankers away from coastal areas until they must approach to enter port. There is also the need to ensure that very large vessels are controlled by highly skilled personnel with an understanding of the problems encountered during a voyage. This involves organizing training programmes to fit the crew for the task. However, though in some countries this can be achieved by the national shipping industry, there are others without the necessary resources and infrastructure to implement such a programme. Only by international agreement can pressure be brought to bear and help extended to all shipping companies in the effort to make sure that whatever flag the ship flies, safety standards and trained manpower levels are adequate to prevent accidents.

## Corrosion

There have been incidents where failures within the ship's structure have resulted in pollution and explosions. There is less steel weight per deadweight tonne in large tankers than in other ships which means that their structures are prone to corrosion. To combat this problem the tanks are coated with substances that reduce the steel oil interface and in many cases higher grade steel and other compounds are used.

## The Ships

V.L.C.C.'s and U.L.C.C.'s are in many ways very simple ships from the nature of cargo they are designed to carry. There is no need for separation between grades of cargo as they carry full cargoes of crude oil from the loading port to the port of discharge. The ship has no real need to segregate the cargo into many different tanks; the size of individual tanks is dominated by the need for strength and adherence to bulk-head rules. The pipeline system is uncomplicated — on many ships there are only sluice valves in the after bulkhead of each tank, with suction from the aftermost tank.

The problems posed by operating and building large tankers have been largely solved by the shipping industry by the application of technological innovations and in the institution of more efficient practices. In many respects (despite the problems) these ships are still the safest and most economic means of moving vast quantities of oil from production sites to the consuming areas of the world.

### FURTHER READING

Baptist, C., *Tanker Handbook for Deck Officers*, Brown Son & Ferguson, Glasgow, 1981.

Dewry, H.P., *The Impact of New Tanker Regulations*, H.P. Dewry Marine Publications, Shipping Study No. 94, London, 1981.

I.M.O., Crude Oil Washing Systems, No. 80.11.E., I.M.O., London, 1978.

I.M.O., *Inert Gas Systems for Oil Tankers*, No. 80.15.E., I.M.O., London, 1979.

Rutherford, D., *Tanker Cargo Handling*, Charles Griffin & Co Ltd., London, 1980.

# 9 Product Carriers

## Products Handled

The method of carrying, handling and managing the distribution of petroleum products is much more complex than that of crude oil.

Petroleum products are the end result of the refining or production phase of the oil industry and are used extensively either as feed stock for various industrial processes or for direct consumption as energy to drive the world's industry and transport. Generally these products are classified under three main headings; black oils, clean oils and chemicals.

- Black oils are the residues from the refining process and are generally of higher specific gravities than clean oils. Often their viscosity and pour point requires that they be heated before they can be pumped and handled efficiently. They are generally treated as dirty cargoes which can pose long term pollution problems. Heating, in tankers carrying these products, is provided by steam carrying pipes that run through the cargo hold. Generally, black oils do not give off explosive gases and are therefore, comparatively safe to handle.
- Clean oils are the distilate fractions from the refining process: they are corrosive to mild steel and give off explosive gases. The pour point and viscosity are such that these products do not need heating. They can be dangerous to handle because of the explosive nature of the gas emissions when mixed with oxygen so there is a need for the adherence to stringent safety measures. These cargoes are liable to contamination from the ship's structure and their high value necessitates the use of tank coatings to cut down tank corrosion.
- Chemicals are highly corrosive to the usual materials used in ship building and can be highly dangerous when mixed. They require specialised substances in tank construction, highly expensive tank coatings and an extensive system of separation between tanks and

pipeline systems carrying incompatible products in the same ship. Chemical carriage is a very specialised trade needing highly skilled and trained crews and specifically designed and constructed vessels.

One hazard common to all products carriers is the mixing of different grades when loading, discharging or carrying cargoes; the hazard increases the "cleaner" the oil grade.

Differences in specific gravity of grades make it very difficult to design the "optimum" ship — one that will carry a range of oil-related products. Clean oils, because of their low specific gravity, need a *volume limited vessel* — that is one where as much volume as possible can be carried per deadweight tonne: black oil ships tend to be deadweight limited.

## Product Carriers

Product carriers can be designed specifically to carry black or clean oils or they can be designed to carry black and clean oils on separate voyages (after a thorough cleaning of the cargo tanks before swapping from one to the other). It is not a normal practice to carry black oils and clean oils at the same time in the same ship. The main criteria used when designating a ship clean or black, is the type of hold protection against corrosion of the hold structure. This protection entails coating the hold structure and bulkheads with some form of corrosion inhibiting material. When changing from clean to black oils or vice versa, extensive tank cleaning is necessary to negate the possibility of contamination by residues of a particular product remaining in the tank before loading a different one.

## Trading Patterns

As discussed earlier, the purpose of the products carrier is to carry refined products from the oil refineries to the consumer. There are four likely voyage patterns all of which tend to be intra-regional, that is, within the local hinterland of the refinery base. Because voyage lengths tend to be short there is no need for extensive bunker facilities on vessels specifically designed for this trade. The trading patterns can be grouped in the following way.

- Extensive distribution of refined products from one refinery to another to enable blending and further processing to take place.
- Distribution of large parcels of products to storage terminals where consumer distribution schedules and order processing can be undertaken.
- Direct distribution of small parcels from refinery to consumer terminals.
- Distribution of small parcels from storage terminals to consumer premises according to the order processing cycle.

In many areas of the world there are severe limits to the design size of product carriers caused by the position and capacity of the discharge terminal (criteria for the construction and design of terminals being the amount of usage they receive rather than the technology of ships on the route). Such shore facilities were built at the same time as production infrastructure and were, therefore, matched to the technology available at that time. The cost of updating the terminal can only be justified if increases in efficiency result in positive returns on investment.

Limited terminal capacity has led the product operator to adopt a multi-port itinerary for their ships in an effort to utilize the economic advantages inherent in using larger vessels. Discharge terminal capacity dictates the size of 'parcel' that can be accepted which is in turn a product of the throughput of a given commodity within the production process.

## Ship Cargo Arrangements

Product carriers are often expected to deliver a number of different grades of oil to the same customer on the same voyage as well as carrying parcels of oil for subsequent customers. The ships concerned must be very flexible in their arrangement of cargo tanks in order that carriage, loading and discharge can be accomplished without mixing the different grades and safe passage is assured. Loading and discharge order must enable draft limitations to be observed throughout the voyage. In total, it means that the ships must be able to vary the size of parcels carried on different voyages and meet the needs of multi-port discharge (see Figure 9.1).

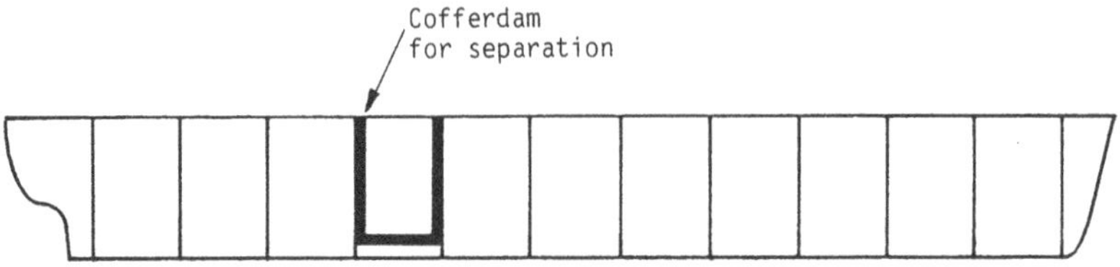


FIGURE 9.1. Chemical products carrier

If more than one product is carried on the same voyage the ship must be designed to enable the parcels to be kept separate — especially during loading and discharge when the greatest danger of contamination occurs. This can be achieved by what is known as segregation or separation. The former demands that in any foreseen circumstances there is *complete* isolation of one product from another. The only way to achieve this is to have a separate pump and piping system for each grade of cargo and to construct the ship such that no pipe carrying one grade passes through a tank containing another. This arrangement can be designed, (as we shall see when we discuss chemical carriers later in the chapter) but is relatively expensive and increases eventual carrying costs. Separation is the normal method employed — cargo capacity is separated into product areas throughout the ship and there are at least two closed valves between each cargo grade. All tanks are kept oil tight so that there is no possibility of one grade leaking into another. The more tanks there are in the ship the greater the number of pipelines, the greater the number of pipeline paths and isolated sections of cargo capacity that need to be separated. For the majority of product carriers, four pumps and piping systems are adequate for normal operations. If more than four grades are carried, there is a need during loading and discharge to pass different grades along the same stretch of pipelines. A hierarchy of contamination effects has been built up in order that products with the highest contamination risk are passed along the pipeline first and the cargoes which are less vulnerable to contamination are passed through last.

## Hold Structure Protection

The central concern of any shipowner is the need to keep the ship in working order. This is achieved either by planned maintenance or by preventative measures designed to prolong the asset's life. The two prime considerations for the product carrier operator when approaching this desire are:

- To maintain at all times the physical properties of the cargo when in the care of the ship's crew, making sure that there is no contamination from other parcels or from the corrosion of the ship's structure
- To protect the ship's structure from the corrosive effect of the products carried and so maintain its asset value.

Which method is adopted depends on the age of the ship and the philosophy of the company. The ship's tank can be coated with some form of corrosion protection that is compatible with the likely range of products to be carried or the tanks can be left uncoated and the corrosive destruction of the structure accepted. Of course, for some grades of cargo the shipowner has no choice but to coat the tanks as the product resulting from corrosion can contaminate certain grades of oil. Once again, the answer is partly a matter of economics in that the method chosen must be in respect of return on investment. The properties of coatings and oil products are well known to the industry so it is relatively simple to establish which coating is compatible with which product. The costs of coating a ship's tank or of leaving the tank uncoated can be clearly established; the expensive long-term method can be calculated against maintenance costs. It must be acknowledged that although coating cuts down the costs of maintaining the ship structure, costs are incurred in maintaining the coating itself.

When considering whether to coat the tank or not, consideration has to be given to the changing nature of the protection needed over the life of the ship. In the short term the coating will have to withstand the rotation of various grades of oil and water ballast, a range of temperatures in the cargo, the pressure of water used to clean the tanks and the effect of inert gas. In the long term consideration will have to be given to future changes in product mix and new products demanding changed carrying environments.

## Chemical Carriers

Ships designed to carry a range of chemicals in bulk are derived directly from product carriers. Indeed when chemicals were first transported in bulk, (as opposed to drums on general cargo ships) converted products carriers were used. A very brief note on a few of the vast range of chemicals carried at sea will give an indication of the problems that must be solved when designing ships for this type of trade.

- Ammonia is used in making fertiliser and other industrial products, gives off a colourless gas with a suffocating smell and can cause irritation to the eyes and skin. There is a moderate explosion hazard present in the vicinity of the gas, especially when exposed to a naked light in an enclosed space. Storage vessels can be constructed of mild steel with very little corrosion taking place, but, ammonia quickly corrodes copper and copper alloys, aluminium and aluminium alloys, galvanised surfaces, polyester resins or P.V.C.; these last often being the base for tank coatings.
- Caustic soda is used in many chemical processes. It does not give off any vapour but is highly corrosive. When in contact with aluminium or zinc a chemical reaction takes place which results in the release of hydrogen that in itself is very inflammable. Mild steel is suitable for storage with very little corrosion taking place; however, it will be noted that after discharge the surface is effectively cleaned. The tank structures are often coated with epoxy resin. Caustic soda reacts very dangerously when mixed with certain other chemicals and must therefore be isolated from other parcels of cargo.
- Nitric acid is a feed stock for the manufacture of fertilisers, explosives, dyes and drugs. It is not flammable but gives off a choking odour. There is a severe explosion hazard when in contact with organic material and precautions must be taken to isolate any chance of this occurring. It is usually stored in stainless steel, glass or P.T.F.E. containers but causes damage to brass, bronze, polyethylene and P.V.C.
- Phospheric acid is used to manufacture fertilizers, soaps and detergents and is a colourless liquid with very little odour. High grade stainless steels or mild steel coated with rubber are the main materials used for containers. This product is highly corrosive to most ferrous

based metals thus the need for coatings or only high grade stainless steels.

- Propylene is used as a base for the manufacture of other chemicals and gives off a colourless gas with a slight odour. It can be carried in containers made of most metals as it does not corrode and has little chemical reaction.

## The Ships

The above brief description of a sample range of the chemicals carried in bulk illustrates the problems inherent in designing and operating tankers in this sector of the industry. The ships must be very sophisticated in order to make carriage and handling of the cargo acceptably safe. Very often the parcels of cargo are relatively small and to maintain reasonable utilisation of cargo carrying capacity, provision must be made for a large number of tanks of a small size. These must be constructed using a variety of materials and sometimes incorporate coatings on their interior surfaces. If the vessel is designed for a particular type or range of products, the specification for the design of the ship can be easily prepared: for a ship intended for a more open trading pattern, due regard must be paid to the demand for chemical carriage with the subsequent design incorporating as much flexibility as possible to enable safe carriage of all likely products.

Cargo carrying capacity must be divided in such a way, that on the same voyage, liquids which are highly corrosive, inflammable, toxic or explosive can be carried without endangering the ship's structure, the operating personnel or the outside environment and in such a condition that the risk of cross contamination of one chemical by another is minimised. In many cases, mixing one chemical with another, (apart from the economic penalty caused by altering the physical characteristics of the delivered product) result in grave hazards to the ship, the crew and the environment.

Chemical carriers by operating on multi-port discharge itineries bring problems of cargo stowage in that draft/trim criteria must be maintained throughout the voyage. Therefore, a very complex ship design is required, the highest priority being safety, but with the need for the flexibility demanded by trading patterns. The ships will have a large number of discharge lines, pumps and cofferdams between tanks and certain tanks will have to be completely isolated from the rest of the cargo system — these being loaded directly from the tank top and discharged using portable immersed pumps.

## The I.M.O. Code

The nature and dangers posed by the type of products carried by chemical tankers is such that I.M.O. have published a *Code for the Construction and Equipment of Ships carrying Dangerous Chemicals in Bulk.*

The basic aim of the code is stated in the preamble:

> The code has been devised and developed to provide international standards for the safe carriage of dangerous chemicals in bulk by outlining the desired construction standards for such ships and the equipment that they should carry. The U.S. publication 'Evaluation of the Hazards of bulk water transportation of industrial chemicals' was used as a base guide to drawing up the code.

The purpose of the code is,

> to recommend suitable design criteria, construction standards and other safety measures for ships transporting chemical substances in bulk so as to minimise the risk to the ship, its crew and the neighbourhood.

The hazards considered in the code are grouped into five main categories: fire, health, water pollution, air pollution and reactivity. The code is regularly updated and reviewed in the light of technological development. The code's basic assumption is that the nature of the products carried and the hazards these products pose have direct effects on the methods of construction, the materials used in the tank structure and on operational techniques. There is a need, therefore, for an international organization to lay down minimum requirements for the standard of containment necessary to protect the environment in the event of a collision or the ship running aground. The code classifies chemical carriers into three groups based on the hazards associated with the various chemicals each is likely to carry:

- Type one ships are for those designed to carry cargoes which-pose the greatest hazards and thus need the greatest care, especially related to the external environment in the case of an accident
- Type two ships are for those cargoes which pose some danger but are not considered to require type one protection
- Type three ships are for those cargoes which need only moderate degrees of containment.

The specifications are based on the expected nature of damage sustained in the event of an accident that results in a fracture of the ship's hull. The idea is to arrange the tanks containing the most hazardous commodities as far away from the hull structure as is consistent with good design, thus making the escape of these chemicals extremely unlikely. The code also contains criteria regarding the stability of the ship once the hull has been damaged and the need for the vessel to remain afloat.

The general recommendations for all ships lay down rules for the separation of the cargo spaces from the engine room and non-cargo spaces by cofferdams or pumprooms. Any commodity that reacts dangerously with other substances must be carried in tanks that are separated from other cargo areas both around the tank and through any gas venting system. These cargoes must have separate pipeline and pumping systems.

To protect the crew, all accommodation should be aft and not built over cargo carrying spaces. In inert gas or liquid blanket should be used to control the atmosphere in the tanks if liable to be dangerous to the ship or the crew.

The code is not mandatory; it is brought into force by individual national governments passing the provisions into national law by legislation.

There are a mass of other Regulations contained in I.M.O. conventions concerned with operational and handling standards, loading and discharge procedures, ballast and tank washing discharges, survey and record keeping regulations and ship repairs.

The carriage of petroleum parcels is a very complex and sophisticated process which can, at times, be highly dangerous to the ship, the crew and the surrounding environment. The high standards required of both ships and crew have led to much research and development in ship design, materials for construction and personnel training. The research involves many branches of science and engineering in producing solutions to the problems and a highly trained workforce to operate the technical system in a safe and economic manner.

**Liquid Gas Carriers**

The carriage of gases by ship for use in energy generation or as a feed stock for the petro-chemical industry is of very recent origin; indeed, it only commenced in any quantities in the 1950's. Vessels designed for this type of carriage, transport the gases in liquified form in specially constructed tanks. There are two methods used, each of which fits a particular situation that is dependent to a great extent on the type of gas.

In the first method, the gas is shipped in bottles or cylinders at up to two times atmosphere pressure, at which the gas becomes a liquid and can be handled like petroleum. The second method leaves the gas at atmospheric pressure but lowers the temperature below boiling, thus liquifying the gas.

For the purpose of this study, hydrocarbon gas can be categorised under two main headings — petroleum gas and natural gas. The first is a product of the refining process, the second is either found in pockets in the earth or mixed with crude oil and is collected at the oil fields, thus the name, "natural".

**Liquid Petroleum Gas**

The term L.P.G., (Liquid Petroleum Gas) covers all those gases resulting from the refining process (for example butane and propane). These were the first gases to be transported in bulk safely and economically. L.P.G. is carried in pressurised containers sometimes aided by refrigeration to liquify the gas. In many countries there have been regulations passed by the government covering the storage and carriage of L.P.G. represented in the U.K. by a safety code.

L.P.G. can be a very dangerous cargo to handle. Most petroleum gases have a gas to liquid volume ratio of over 200; that is the gas will occupy a volume 200 times that of a similar mass of liquid. Any leakage of the liquid from a tank can result in a very large volume of gas in the air which can easily be ignited. The container must be constructed and maintained to the highest standards to prevent, as far as is possible, such an escape. The vapour is heavier than air so will flow along the deck, displacing any air in drains or low lying spaces; it tends to disperse slowly, especially if the air is still.

Ship Classification Societies lay down specific design criteria for the carriage of L.P.G. The rules cover materials and methods used in the construction of pressure vessels, the access points into the vessels, the gas tightness of the hull and the means for determining the temperature of the liquid and the level the liquid reaches in the tank.

**Loading and Discharge**

L.P.G. is loaded or discharged through pipelines that run along the upper deck from the shore connection to the tops of the pressure vessels. The simplest method is to use the gas pressure to push the liquid into or out of the tank by connecting one line for gas vapour and one for the liquid. The loading sequence follows the following pattern. The liquid line is opened and the pressure of the vapour on the liquid in the shore storage tank pushes the L.P.G. into the ship's tank. As the liquid level in the ship's tank rises, the gas at the top of the tank is pressurised; when the pressure in the ship and shore tanks is almost equal, a gas compressor is used to pump gas along the gas line into the tank ashore, thus maintaining a pressure differential between the shore and the ship. This pressure is maintained until the ship's tank is full. Discharge is achieved by reversing the process and maintaining a higher pressure in the ship.

Measurement of the liquid in the tank causes problems but these are overcome by using sound generating equipment. Sound travels at different speeds through the liquid and the gas and the resultant speed differential can be used to measure the depth of liquid.

**Liquid Natural Gas**

Liquid Natural Gas (L.N.G.) is primarily methane which boils at the very low temperature of −162°C and therefore causes technical problems in transportation.

As non-renewable sources of raw material becomes scarce, (especially oil) methane rapidly gains in importance in terms of world energy and now accounts for approximately 17% of all consumption. Sea transport of methane gas over long distances is relatively new and until it became both technically and economically feasible to move it, the majority was flared off at the well head, causing oil fields to have that characteristic red, flickering glow at night as a result of the flames at the top of the venting towers. For a non-renewable energy source, this was extremely wasteful, (some would say criminal) but until a method was developed to transport the gas from the oil fields to the consumer at a price that was competitive with other forms of energy, there was no real alternative.

The technical problems are formidable both from the angle of engineering knowledge and shipping economics. There were several questions that had to be answered before the ships came into service, for example how to transport a commodity that must remain at a temperature of less than 162°C for all of the voyage if it is to remain a liquid. At this temperature the usual materials used in ship construction become extremely brittle and liable to crack if moved too violently. The solution to this problem must be the use of suitable materials: however, in many cases, such materials are much more expensive to use. Is it best to keep the gas cool on board by a liquification plant and machinery or rely on some form of insulation and small boil off of gas to keep the required temperature? Is it possible to liquefy enough gas at source as the gas fills a volume of 600 times that of an equivalent weight of liquid and still deliver an economical product at the end of the voyage? Methane has a very high calorific value; that is it will produce more heat from a given volume than coal gas and can be supplied to consumers through a pipeline network. As the cost to consumers of other forms of energy increases against their diminishing supply, there is an incentive to use methane to help spread the demand for energy across a number of sources.

The solution to the problems of transportation outlined above, was to site the liquification plants at the loading ports and transport the gas in liquid form in large insulated tanks on board ship. Insulated tanks keep the gas cool and allow a certain amount of boil off without the need for refrigerated plant. The liquification plant ashore has to accomplish several tasks before the gas can be transported safely and economically by ship.

- All water and impurities have to be removed to avoid the chance of the gas solidifying around particles in the tank and damaging the tank walls and related equipment.
- Any gas that may solidify at higher temperatures than −162°C must be removed.
- Any remaining methane gas must be cooled to its liquid state and stored to await the arrival of the ship.

Again, it is important to realize that the shipping company, in effect, supply an insulated thermos flask for the transport of the gas with no means for refrigerating the cargo once on board. The gas, therefore, must be in a transportable state when the ship arrives at the load port.

### The Ships

There are two major systems developed to transport liquid gas at the temperatures so low that they are a hazard to the ship's structure. The main consideration is in insulating the tank from the rest of the hull structure in order that the mild steel plating is not cooled into the brittle region, and to structure the tank to make expansion and contraction possible without straining the fabric (see Figure 9.2).

Self-supporting tanks are independently constructed and are lowered into position within the ship on limited anchorage points attached to but insulated from the hull. The tanks have their own internal strength and can expand and contract virtually independently of the ship's hull. The space between individual tanks and the tanks and the ship's hull, is filled with layers of balsa wood and insulating foam; this prevents low temperatures affecting the hull material.

Membrane tanks are constructed of plates that have a very low expansion coefficient. The membrane which is attached to the ship's hull, forms a flexible seal between the liquid gas and the layers of insulation. All static and dynamic forces, produced by the mass of liquid and its movement during the voyage, are transmitted through the insulation to the ship's structure which means that the tanks are an integral part of the ship having no intrinsic strength of their own.

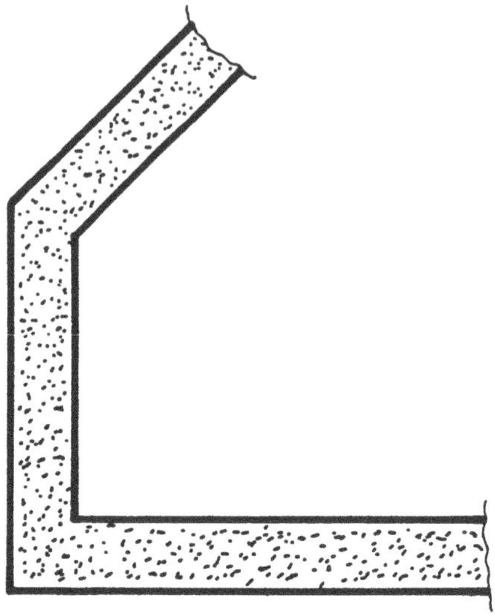

a) Membrane system

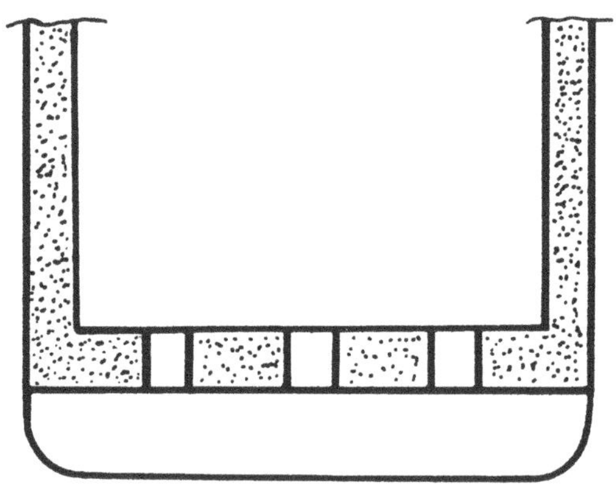

b) Self supporting tanks

FIGURE 9.2. Insulation systems on gas carriers

**Loading and Discharging**

The L.N.G. loading and discharge process is in many ways similar to that of L.P.G. Two pipelines are connected to the tank top, one for liquid and one for vapour. The liquid line is used when loading commences to circulate a small quantity of liquid around the tank to cool the structure by evaporation. Once the temperature is low enough, the main volume of liquid is pumped into the tank, pushing any vapour from the tank along the vapour line to be re-liquified in the plant ashore. No liquification plant exists on board so a certain proportion of the cargo will "boil off" during the voyage; this can be either vented into the atmosphere by using pressure release valves, or, burnt as fuel in the ship's boilers (which have been designed for this purpose). The latter is economically attractive as it reduces the amount of fuel oil used and does not waste the gas.

Discharge is by specifically designed submersible pumps fitted into the bottom of the tanks. Normally, some liquid is left in each to keep the structure cool on the ballast voyage; this reduces expansion and strain on those tanks when loading and helps to speed the loading process and cut down on the quality of gas needed to circulate around the tanks to cool them.

**Operation**

Liquid gas transportation is regarded as a complete system comprising liquification plant, loading/discharge complex and gas carriers. It is capital intensive and there is little speculative building of ships to serve this trade — gas carrier costs roughly twice as much to build as a similar sized tanker. The system is a product of the contracted volume of gas to be moved which in turn affects the size of the liquification plant, port complex and vessel. Thus it is usual to design a ship for a specific trade route and have the ship fixed on a long term contract to serve that route. One problem this sets for the shipping industry is when to order the gas carriers as ship design and construction time scale is about half that of the shore plants. Several shipowners have taken delivery of their gas carriers only to have them laid up whilst awaiting the completion of the other parts of the system.

## FURTHER READING

Baptist, C., *Tanker handbook for Deck Officers*, Brown Son and Ferguson, Glasgow, 1981.

Dewry, H.P., *The Products Tanker Fleet*, Shipping Study No. 96, H.P. Dewry Marine Publications, London, 1981.

Dewry, H.P., *The Growth of the Chemical Carrier Fleet*, Shipping Study No. 90, H.P. Dewry Marine Publications, London, 1980.

Dewry, H.P., *L.N.G. Shipping in the Eighties*, Shipping Study No. 82, H.P. Dewry Marine Publications, London, 1978.

Fairplay, Chemical Tankers, the Ships and the Market, Fairplay Publications, London, 1981.

I.M.O., *Code for the Construction and Equipment of Ships Carrying Dangerous Chemicals in Bulk*, No. 80.13.E., I.M.C.O., London, 1981.

I.M.O., Code for the Construction and Equipment of *Ships carrying Liquified Gases in Bulk*, No. 80.14.E., I.M.C.O., London, 1981.

# 10 The Future

This book has stressed that in seeking technological solutions to economic and operational problems, the shipping industry has tended to specialize — each ship type is designed to transport a narrow range of cargoes in order to be more efficient than its competitors. This can be seen in the move to containerisation, (needing a highly developed infrastructure), bulk carriers designed to carry a particular commodity and crude oil tankers (unsuitable for products carriage).

Against this general trend, there have been attempts to design, construct and operate ships that are flexible in relation to the cargoes they carry. There are ships designed to carry liquid and dry bulk cargoes on alternative voyages, to carry containers, dry bulk and packages and ships designed to carry liquid cargoes and containers.

The need for multi-purpose ships arises from two unrelated factors. The fundamental problem with both oil transport and dry bulk carriage is that the raw materials carried are used in manufacturing industry or power generation in places removed from their source. Most of the world's raw materials are found in areas with low populations and subsequently, little need for industry; thus very limited demand for large imports of other bulk commodities. Even when there is an expanding economy in primary source areas such as some oil producing states, imports tend to be manufactured goods, which are unsuitable for carriage in tankers. The trade to developing countries tends to be similarly imbalanced with basic products exported and manufactured goods imported.

The imbalance of trade between a country and its markets or suppliers means that in an increasingly cargo-specialized shipping industry, the technology pertaining to one leg of the trade route does not permit the carriage of commodities on the return leg — ships designed to carry large volumes of crude oil, one type of dry bulk cargo or containers exclusively are fully loaded on only one leg of the route and must return empty before loading another cargo. This, in theory, means that these types of ship can spend up to 50% of their productive time in ballast or with empty containers. The freight earned on one leg must, therefore, be enough to operate the ship over two voyages. As has been shown, for the tanker owner or bulk carrier operator within the *open market*, (where the laws of supply and demand apply) the supply of ships and cargoes at any given time has a direct effect on earnings. If there are many ships and few cargoes, the freight rates are low. It is attractive to the ship owner, therefore, to have a vessel available that can carry more than one type of cargo. The container ship owner has a different problem: he must match the technology used on the majority of his trade routes with a route that does not demand that technology.

These factors combined, have led shipowners and naval architects to research and develop a solution to the problem of productivity of certain ship types on certain trade routes. The major underlying need has stemmed from the desire on the part of the ship owner to reduce the non-payload voyages as much as possible. As has been stated in earlier chapters, in the tanker and dry bulk trades it is very difficult to reduce ballast time to zero as there is very little scope for carrying oil one way and dry bulk the other. In other words, the ideal trade route for any ship designed to carry either oil or dry bulk would be one where a country export oil to another and imports dry bulk from the same source. This type of trade route would be perfect for the employment of a fleet of combined dry bulk/oil ships.

## Justification for Combined Carriers

In order to discuss the need for more flexible ships on certain of the world's trade routes, the following section looks at the justification put forward by the shipping industry for the design and operation of combined ore, bulk, oil carriers (O.B.O.) or ore, oil carriers (O.O.). These ships are designed to carry either oil or dry bulk on separate voyages, at different times, and are potentially more productive than a pure tanker or bulk carrier.

In making the decision to invest in combined carrier tonnage as opposed to a pure oil carrier or a dry bulk carrier, the shipowner is presented with two possible operating scenarios. He can either combine voyages over a period by carrying dry bulk and oil in a sequence that keeps ballast passages to a minimum or he can switch his ship between the dry bulk and the oil market sectors, (in response to freight rate changes) and thus earn the greatest possible return on his investment. It must always be borne in mind when taking these decisions that a combined carrier costs approximately 10% more to build and operate than a pure tanker or bulk carrier of similar size and tonnage. It is imperative therefore that the ship has, at the very least, to utilize its payload capacity for the minimum of 60% of its operating life to earn the same return as that for the tanker or bulk carrier. The independent shipowner seeks to maximize his earnings by operating ships, therefore he must adapt management performance to combine flexibility with greater earning power.

### Combined Voyages

The operation of combined voyages seeks to mix short ballast passages with longer loaded ones. The following example of a round the world sequence of voyages involving both oil carriage and dry bulk shipments illustrates how this can be accomplished.

- Starting in Peru, the ship loads ore and carries this to Japan across the Pacific Ocean. After discharge and cleaning, ballast is loaded and the ship sails for the Arabian Gulf. In the Gulf, oil is loaded and the ship proceeds to N.W. Europe via the Cape. After discharge, a short ballast voyage is undertaken to N. Africa to load a cargo of oil for the U.S. West Coast. After discharge and ballasting in the U.S. the ship sails for Peru and thus completes the worldwide sequence of voyages and is ready to start again. This shows how it is possible to utilize the design capability of the ship to keep ballast passages to a minimum.

It takes a different management style and effort, to negotiate a series of contracts that will keep the ship employed, to that normally found in bulk shipping companies. The use of contracts where the ship is not named in the document — but a promise is given to deliver the fixed amounts of cargo in given time periods — makes it possible to plan the schedules of a fleet of this type of ship. Management has a greater degree of flexibility than for *spot market* operations or individual ship contracts and also has a stable environment in which to operate. The problem may be encountered where the cargo owner may offer a lower freight rate than that currently found in the spot market, in exchange for this type of commitment.

## Spot Market Operations

The operation of the spot market, that is one voyage contracts at the prevailing freight rate, is how most tramp ship owners have earned their living. It does not seem too far fetched to suggest that these shipowners should see the combined carrier as an extension of their trading pattern, enabling them to extend their opportunities from one market to the other. The switching of the combined carrier from oil to dry bulk according to which market offers the highest freight rates is seen as a method of maximizing earnings. At first sight, this possibility must be attractive to owners who have spent their working lives ensuring that their ships are always available to load cargoes wherever the return is greatest. There are, however, some grave drawbacks to this approach.

The basic assumption underlying this philosophy is that the shipping markets follow a pattern which enables the time when it is advantageous to transfer the combined carrier from oil trading to dry bulk trading to be calculated. This means that when tanker rates are high, the ship is traded in the oil market as a tanker, but when this rate falls, there comes a time when the dry bulk rate will be higher; it is then profitable to transfer to dry bulk trading.

Obviously, the optimum conditions to suit this type of trading would occur if the rate structures were counter cyclical, that is, with tanker rates high, bulk rates low and vice versa. This is only theoretically possible. Freight rates in the tanker market and the dry bulk market tend to follow closely the performance of the world economy. Thus, at times of economic growth, manufacturing industry increases the demand for raw materials and energy, which in turn causes a rise in the demand for sea transport. There is a subsequent rise in freight rates in both the dry bulk and the tanker market, the steepness of which, (and its high point) will, to a large extent, depend upon how quickly shipping supply can adjust to shipping demand. This does mean that, at most times, the dry bulk and tanker market rates follow a similar trend: this makes the switching of ships between market sectors rather a waste of time. There is also the depressive effect on rates of a pool of tonnage ready to transfer whenever rates are rising.

### Events Affecting Combined Carrier Utilisation

Three major factors have played a part in distorting the theoretical basis for investment in combined carriers once they have come on to the market. These factors clearly illustrate the difficulty involved in applying theoretical criteria in a practical environment.

- The closure of the Suez Canal led to an upsurge in chartering activity within the oil market to carry the oil demanded by N.W. Europe around Southern Africa. This activity in turn caused freight rates to soar to unheard of levels and attracted the owners of combined tonnage into the oil sector. These shipowners found it highly profitable to keep their tonnage in the oil sector, and therefore operate the ships as if they were pure tankers. No attempt was made to use the inherent flexibility of a combined carrier to reduce ballast voyages and maximize profits. In the period after the Canal closure, as much as 80% of combined tonnage was being traded exclusively in carrying oil cargoes. This, in effect, meant that though the owner was making profits, he was foregoing the extra profit that could have been earned with a pure tanker of similar size and had no justification for building a combined carrier in the first place.
- The oil crisis of 1973 caused a severe slump in freight rates in the oil sector and a combined carrier owner found that the 10% extra costs involved in operating his ships soon made these ships vulnerable in the oil trade. They turned anew to try and investigate how the flexibility of their ships could more fully exploit inherent cost saving capabilities. That large numbers of combined carriers are laid up in the present slump seems to indicate that market swapping as opposed to carefully planned scheduling is not the best way to operate the vessels.
- The 1960's and 1970's saw dry bulk traffic grow rapidly but the size of the individual consignments expanded. This growth was fuelled by the rapid expansion of the Japanese economy and led to the demand for large bulk carriers. The size of bulk consignments made it economic to combine in one ship the potential to carry both oil and dry bulk. It would not be so economically viable if the relative

sizes of consignments of oil and dry bulk were not similar.

**Ownership**

Ownership of combined carriers is predominantly in the hands of independent shipowners as most of the large oil or ore companies are limited to trading in one particular commodity and have no need for the versatility offered by the combined carrier. Independent owners have the management skills and the incentive to earn significant returns on their investment.

**The Ships**

In appearance, the ships are similar to ore carriers with the engines aft and wide, heavy hatch covers. There are two sub-groups of vessel, namely the Oil, Bulk, Ore Carrier (O.B.O.) and the Ore, Oil Carrier (O.O.) (see Figure 10.1).

The O.B.O. has a similar cross-sectional area to that of the general purpose bulk carrier: indeed, they are in direct competition with each other when the O.B.O. is operating in the dry bulk trades. There are obvious differences which make an O.B.O. more expensive than a general purpose carrier to build. The main holds are designed to carry both dry bulk and liquid cargoes and their sides are smooth in order to facilitate the discharge of dry cargo. Webs and strength members are enclosed in a double skin to leave the bulkheads and sides flush; this aids cleaning when switching from one commodity to the other. The hatch covers must be fairly wide for discharging ore and oil and gas tight for the carriage of oil. The oil cargo lines are carried in a *trunking* and a pumproom is housed forward of the engine room.

The O.O. vessel is designed to carry heavy ores in its mid-section holds with oil-tight wing tanks to be used for ballast or oil cargoes. A deep double bottom raises the centre of gravity of the ore and provides space to accommodate the pipeline system.

It is obvious that the combined carrier designer must try and reconcile the sometimes conflicting criteria used when building a pure tanker or bulk carrier. To discharge bulk cargoes requires large hatch openings, which poses problems of gas tightness and safety when

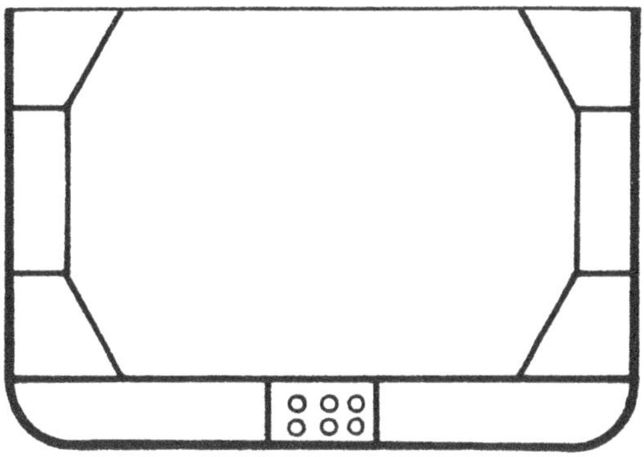

Section through oil/bulk/ore carrier cargo hold

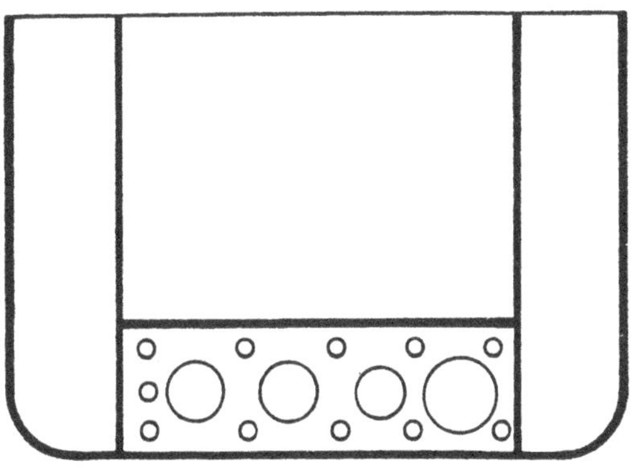

Section through ore/oil carrier cargo hold

FIGURE 10.1. Combination carriers

carrying oil. Hold surfaces need to be flush to facilitate the discharge of dry bulk and cleaning between cargoes but internal strength to take the strain of the movement of liquid cargoes is a necessity. A method must be found to locate pump suctions and valves in the hold bottoms without becoming blocked or damaged when carrying an ore cargo. The ship must be fitted with an effective pipeline and pumping system that will perform as efficiently as one fitted to a tanker of similar size. There must be provision for cargo heating if the ship is not to be restricted in its oil trading and the system used must withstand the loading, carrying and discharge of ore cargoes.

All these extra specifications lead to a more expensive ship and, at times, to potential hazards when undertaking work that is compatible with one type of cargo but not with another. There is the danger that oil or gas may collect in the double bottom space and go undetected until an accident occurs. There have been several unexplained disasters concerning combined carriers which people suspect were caused by repairs to parts of the ship which were initially thought safe but eventually proved hazardous.

## Other Combined Systems

Unit load systems set out to greatly increase the productivity of general cargo carriage and have transformed the methods used to handle individual packages. Containerisation has been physically integrated into most areas of materials handling in the developed countries and has led to a tendency to initiate container services between developed and developing countries. One of the main problems in this is that the type of cargo on offer — especially from the developing to the developed country — is not containerisable. To overcome this difficulty, many ship designers are experimenting with ships that can carry containers on one leg of the voyage and be converted to carry other types of cargo for the other. In the future, more such systems will be developed to meet the particular needs of the trade routes the ships are designed to serve.

## Energy

Almost all commercial merchant ships are powered by oil fed plant. However, the oil crisis of the last few years has highlighted the need to research the likely power plant of the future. Amongst the many options, three alternatives to oil seem to have gained the most attention.

The basis of steam power around the turn of the century was coal which necessitated a worldwide network of coal bunkering points. It is felt by many engineers that coal generation plant could easily be developed for use in ships using some automatic fuel feed system. Australian owners have ordered some coal powered bulk carriers for use on the Australia to Japan trade to carry coal. This route will negate the need for bunker stations as one end of the route is from a coal port. It is feasible to set up a network of coal stations and with more efficient power plant, longer voyages between bunkering can be undertaken. It is possible in the short term for more coal powered ships to be built for special routes which will provide the necessary operating experience for full scale introduction when oil becomes scarce.

Nuclear power has been suggested as a basis for powering merchant ships ever since it became a practice in the world's navies. Several nuclear powered experimental ships have been built but their operation proved to be uncompetitive at the time. One further block to the operation of nuclear powered ships has been legislation in certain countries to ban these ships from entering commercial ports until their safety is assured.

For the romantic observer, the answer to the energy crisis in shipping lies in a return to wind power which is an infinite resource and is seen as returning grace and beauty to a very functional industry. There has been some serious research and the consensus seems to be that in certain circumstances wind assisted power ships may have a role to play.

## Air Competition

Finally, in the future, the question of air competition is going to be of much greater significance. There is no doubt that air has taken a lot of cargo in the high value, low weight area from the shipping industry. In pure transport terms, air transport is very expensive and should not therefore be competitive. There is an awareness in that a comparison of transport costs is not valid and a study of business logistics states that the transport cost is only one of a number of interrelated costs that must be studied when a company looks at its distribution system. If a high transport cost can be offset by sufficient savings in other parts of the logistic system, it is more efficient to use the high cost transport mode. The main advantage of air transport is its speed but this speed can be used to cut down on inventory holding, warehousing and shorten lead times between order and delivery. There is also a feeling that less packaging is needed and that insurance rates are lower. If savings can be made in all these areas, sufficient to offset the high freight charges, firms will increasingly come to look to air for their transport. When planes are designed to take a number of I.S.O. shipping containers, the competition from air will become fierce. The shipping industry must be aware of this source of competition and attempt to provide a service that can compete.

## Conclusion

The move towards specialisation in shipping seems to be at an end as the industry becomes aware that costs are important. An awareness that one way of cutting the costs per unit carried is to design ships that can be heavily utilised throughout their lives cutting out as far as possible ballast passages. The cost of fuel and the possibility of oil becoming scarce points to the use of alternative fuels to power the ships. As business logistics increasingly spreads through the business world, the shipping industry must review its operations so that it can meet the challenge of other modes.

In other areas, the shipping industry, especially in the traditional maritime countries, is in for a turbulent future. There is the insistence of the newly developed countries that they must have a larger say in the shipping services to their countries, the question of flags of convenience and the support for shipping services by individual countries. Shipping is going through a transformation and what the structure will be in the 1990's only time will tell.

# Index